I THINK I HEARD A ROOSTER CROW

Delores Chapman Danley

WestBow
P R E S S
A DIVISION OF THOMAS NELSON

Scripture taken from the Holy Bible, New International Version®. Copyright © 1973, 1978, 1984 Biblica. Used by permission of Zondervan. All rights reserved.

WestBow Press books may be ordered through booksellers or by contacting:

WestBow Press
A Division of Thomas Nelson
1663 Liberty Drive
Bloomington, IN 47403
www.westbowpress.com
1-(866) 928-1240

Because of the dynamic nature of the Internet, any web addresses or links contained in this book may have changed since publication and may no longer be valid. The views expressed in this work are solely those of the author and do not necessarily reflect the views of the publisher, and the publisher hereby disclaims any responsibility for them.

Any people depicted in stock imagery provided by Thinkstock are models, and such images are being used for illustrative purposes only.

Certain stock imagery © Thinkstock.

ISBN: 978-1-4497-1711-7 (sc)
ISBN: 978-1-4497-1712-4 (hc)
ISBN: 978-1-4497-1710-0 (e)

Library of Congress Control Number: 2011928956

Printed in the United States of America

WestBow Press rev. date: 6/15/2011

Table of Contents

INTRODUCTION

For some reason, since my teenage years (very long ago), I have found it easier to express my most intimate feelings in the form of rhymes rather than in prose. About eight years ago, the Lord started sending me words and rhymes with a different kind of message, and I felt that He wanted me to write them down to share with others. It has been a task that has revealed His immense love for me and has comforted me through some of the most trying times of my life. It is amazing how He sends just the words we need to hear at just the right time! This endeavor has also sent me on a more intense journey through His Word, the Bible. He has shown me new meanings to familiar verses. He has also disclosed new meanings to verses that I had read before but had somehow missed what He was trying to tell me through them. Unless otherwise indicated, the scripture verses recorded in this book were taken from the New International Version of our Lord's Word.

Some of the poems are light and intended to bring a smile to the reader's face. Others contain serious messages that might cause the reader to pause and reflect on some areas of life. Many of the poems brought tears to my eyes as the Lord revealed weak points in my character that needed serious attention.

If any one poem helps any one person make it through a difficult day, then my "labor of love" will not have been in vain. I pray that His will be done with this project. May we all try to live our lives so that we will not have to hear that rooster crow!

PSALM 19:14

May the words of my mouth and the meditation of my heart be pleasing in your sight, O LORD, my Rock and my Redeemer.

TIME
WITH
GOD

Mark 6:46

After leaving them, he went up
on a mountainside to pray.

THE NAILS

Ray Boltz wrote a beautiful song entitled "Feel the Nails." Every time I hear it sung, the lyrics make me cry because they remind me of all the times I let Jesus down by my actions and my words---especially by my words. In the book of James we are told that no man can tame the tongue. James 3:6 warns us that *"The tongue also is a fire, a world of evil among the parts of the body. It corrupts the whole person, sets the whole course of his life on fire, and is itself set on fire by hell."*

One morning as I was thinking about the words of that song, I asked God just how I hurt him by the way I act and speak. Almost immediately He began answering that question to my heart as fast as I could write the words on paper. By the time I finally stopped writing, I was beginning to wish I had not asked; but from that experience I obtained what has turned out to be one of my favorite poems that the Lord has sent me. It has touched many people when I have shared it in various settings and has made them stop and take inventory of their words and actions.

I have often identified myself with Peter on the occasion when he denied his Lord and Savior not once, not twice, but three times in a few brief hours. Just a short time earlier he had vowed that he would defend Christ even to the point of death. From the loftiest height of loyalty to the deepest depths of deception Peter fell. In Luke 22:60-62 we learn that *"Peter replied, 'Man, I don't know what you're talking about!' Just as he was speaking, the rooster crowed. The Lord turned and looked straight at Peter. <u>Then</u> Peter remembered the word the Lord had spoken to him: 'Before the rooster crows today, you will disown me three times.' And he went outside and wept bitterly."*

That word *"then"* is very significant in that passage of Scripture. It is so often *after* the fact that we remember and weep bitter tears. How many times do we fall from the highest mountain to the lowest valley in a matter of hours? We can hurt Christ not just by the words we speak but also by the words we don't speak, as God pointed out to me in the words of the following poem. Whether it is sin of commission or sin of omission, it hurts our Lord deeply. As the words of the song "Feel the Nails" point out, "Am I causing Him pain? Then I know I've got to change. I just can't stand the thought of hurting Him."

5

I THINK I HEARD A ROOSTER CROW

When I said that hurtful word
And repeated gossip I had heard
Stating facts I did not know,
Lord, I think I heard a rooster crow.

When I passed someone in need,
But I had no time for one good deed
And no kindness did I show,
Lord, I think I heard a rooster crow.

When I felt that jealous twinge,
Or the flames of greed made my heart singe,
Floods of doubt pulled me below.
Lord, I think I heard a rooster crow.

When I refused to forgive
Though you said I must if I shall live,
But someone had hurt me so,
Lord, I think I heard a rooster crow.

When I blamed and criticized
And I thought my faults were all disguised,
I was in pride's undertow.
Lord, I think I heard a rooster crow.

When I had that evil thought
And in old Satan's trap I got caught,
This world would not let me go.
Lord, I think I heard a rooster crow.

When I took no time to pray
As I hurried to begin my day,
Life just tossed me to and fro.
Lord, I think I heard a rooster crow.

When I missed a chance to share
My testimony and how you care,
Thus that seed I did not sow,
Lord, I think I heard a rooster crow.

Help me, Lord, to do your will.
Keep me aware of how others feel;
From my heart let your love flow.
I don't want to hear that rooster crow.

Luke 22:59-62

About an hour later another asserted, "Certainly this fellow was with him, for he is a Galilean." Peter replied, "Man I don't know what you're talking about!" Just as he was speaking, the rooster crowed. The Lord turned and looked straight at Peter. Then Peter remembered the word the Lord had spoken to him: "Before the rooster crows today, you will disown me three times." And he went outside and wept bitterly.

I'M STILL HERE

When I feel sad and don't know why
And from my heart there comes a sigh
And sorrow seems it's here to stay
Though there's no cause to feel this way

When I should sing but words won't come
And my whole being just feels numb
When I must force my eyes to see
The wonders that He's made for me

When my soul longs for joy and peace
But doubts and fears just will not cease
I plead, "Oh, Savior, please come near!"
I hear Him whisper, "I'm still here."

HEBREWS 13:5-6

Be content with what you have, because God has said, "Never will I leave you; never will I forsake you." So we say with confidence, "The Lord is my helper; I will not be afraid. What can man do to me?"

MY EXCUSES and GOD'S PROMISES

Lord, I see no way out today.
Then God said, "I will make a way."   (Isaiah 30:21)

Lord, if I fail what will I do?
Then God said, "I will not fail you."   (Joshua 1:5)

Lord, I am just a small, weak man.
Then God said, "When you can't, I can." (Ephesians 3:20)

Lord, when I speak, people will laugh.
Then God said, "Speak on My behalf."   (2 Timothy 1:7)

Lord, I have no riches to bring.
Then God said, "I own everything."   (Psalm 50:12b)

Lord, I have too much work to do.
Then God said, "I make time for you."   (Hosea 10:12)

Lord, I'm afraid! It's not safe here.
Then God said, "Love will cast out fear." (1 John 4:18)

Lord, I have sins I can't combat.
Then God said, "I took care of that."   (Hebrews 9:24-28)

Lord, I will need a helping hand.
Then God said, "I will help you stand."   (Romans 14:4)

Lord, to your will I now resign.
Then God said, "Now I'll call you mine." (Romans 8:14)

I SEE GOD

Who says I can't see God? I saw Him just today.
I saw where He had trod as I went on my way.

He stood so very near by my side as I walked,
And I'm sure I could hear His sweet voice as we talked.

I know I saw His face in a cloud high above
As He sent down more grace in sunshine filled with love.

He stood by a flower and smelled its fragrance sweet.
I could sense His power while kneeling at His feet.

I saw Him in the air; I saw Him in the trees.
I know that He was there; I felt Him in the breeze.

He stood near an old man as he limped down the street.
He laughed and played and ran with each child He would meet.

He sat with me today so we could spend some time.
I know I heard Him say He helped me with this rhyme.

I'll see Him here and there though my sight may grow dim.
He's near---He's everywhere. I know that I see Him!

---

1 JOHN 4: 12

No one has ever seen God; but if we love one another,
God lives in us and his love is made complete in us.

THERE ARE NO WORDS

You gave me many gifts on earth,
Blessings that I am just not worth.
So many things I don't deserve
You gave to me without reserve.

But there are no words to express
My joy and peace and happiness.
Words like "thank you" just seem so small
To praise my Lord who's given all.

You knew no words would ever be
Enough for all you've done for me.
From deep inside, my thanks depart,
Silent thanks from a grateful heart.

PSALM 147:1

*Praise the LORD. How good it is to sing praises to our
God, how pleasant and fitting to praise him!*

WHEN GOD IS SILENT

It's quiet here in my front yard
Though I know I should be working.
To leave this place is very hard,
Though my duties I am shirking.
I'm learning to commune with God;
At times we do not need a word.
He is my friend, my staff and rod;
My every thought by Him is heard.
I think that He must take delight
In observing His creation.
He watches every bird take flight---
Tends to every situation.
He does not have to speak aloud
For me to know He's somewhere near.
He very seldom needs a crowd
When He decides to linger here.
It's nice to just sit quietly
Enjoying all the things He's made.
With my Lord sitting next to me,
We watch the evening shadows fade.
There's noise enough that's made by men,
And so much of earth is violent.
There is no sweeter time than when
Our Lord chooses to be silent.

ROMANS 1: 20

*For since the creation of the world God's invisible qualities---his
eternal power and divine nature---have been clearly seen, being
understood from what has been made, so that men are without excuse.*

The Still Small Voice

This morning I sat quietly and heard God's sweet birds sing.
I watched this day unfold and saw the beauty it would bring.
I love these peaceful moments that we share---my God and I.
"Be still and know that I Am God," I hear my Savior sigh.
I cannot describe the feeling that stirs deep in my soul.
I'm bracing for the storms of life when worldly billows roll.
The enemy among us will soon do his very best
To snatch away this sweet, sweet peace and put me to the test.
But he can't win no matter what he dares to throw my way,
Because my Lord and I are walking down this path today.

I KINGS 19:12

*After the earthquake came a fire, but the Lord was not
in the fire. And after the fire came a gentle whisper.*

PSALM 46:10

"Be still, and know that I am God;...."

HIS PRESENCE

When I arose this morning from my nice warm bed,
Things I felt must be done went running through my head.
I had my day all planned---just how and when and where;
Then I paused a moment to bow my head in prayer.
It dawned on me just then that my plans might not be
The same plans that my Father had in store for me.
He knew that I needed more time to visit Him
So He could fill my cup completely to the brim.
For He knew I would need His mercy and His grace
To handle everything that I would have to face.
In this world we all should be messengers of love,
Striving hard each day to be like God up above.
It is not for us to say, though we have a choice.
He sends us out each day to be His hands and voice.
His will I am seeking, and this one thing I know;
God, if you're not with me, then I don't want to go.

EXODUS 33: 15

*Then Moses said to him, "If your Presence does not
go with us, do not send us up from here."*

CHRIST HAD TIME

Christ never met people in need
When he could not find the time
To pause and do a gracious deed
That would make them feel sublime.

And though His years on earth were few
When He walked up Calvary's hill,
So many souls He'd tended to,
As He did his Father's will.

When they came to Him believing
In the power of His name,
Each one knew he'd be receiving
And would be so glad he came.

So when you feel you have too much,
No time to stop and help one,
Remember Jesus paused to touch
And show the love of God's Son.

MARK 1: 41

*Filled with compassion, Jesus reached
out his hand and touched the man....*

I FELT YOU THERE

I felt you there as darkness filled the hour.
I felt your love, compassion, strength and power.
I felt your peace in the midst of my storm,
And in life's coldness, I felt you keep me warm.

I felt you there as Satan came against me.
I felt you as my shield from threats I could not see.
I felt you lift me up when I slipped and fell,
And in each sickness, I felt you make me well.

I felt your courage when life made me afraid.
I felt your patience with every mess I made.
I felt your presence as a loved one went to you,
And at that time, I felt your comfort see me through.

I feel you every morning when I awake.
I feel you watching every move I make.
I feel you listening as I bow down in prayer.
In each moment of my life, I feel you there.

PSALM 34:15

*The eyes of the Lord are on the righteous and
his ears are attentive to their cry.*

LISTEN

Father, did you speak to me when my mind was so occupied
I did not even notice that you were standing by my side?
Were my thoughts so full of myself; should I hang my head in shame?
Did I miss the gentle whisper when your lips called out my name?

Did you try to speak to my heart to remind me of your love?
Did you wish to light my path today with blessings from above?
Could I not feel your love so near and all the power in it?
Could I not spare some time for you---one hour or one minute?

Did you have some work for me to do, some kindness I should show
To a burdened soul just passing by with shoulders stooping low?
Or did you want to have a chat and spend some time together
Just talking about this great world---the birds, the beasts, the weather?

We should not expect your presence near only when there's trouble,
Or wait to have a talk with you when life's a pile of rubble.
We should be listening for your voice, and answer when you call
And listen when you speak to us---it's an honor above all.

*ISAIAH **66:4***

*"...For when I called, no one answered,
when I spoke, no one listened...."*

THANKS

As I think of the blessings you've sent
And the hours you've lovingly spent
Watching me as I've traveled life's way,
"Thank you" is just not enough to say.

For all the times you've heard every sigh
And held me when I needed to cry
And led me through a most painful day,
"Thank you" is just not enough to say.

For all the times, when filled with despair,
I've run to you and bowed down in prayer
And felt you take my pain all away,
"Thank you" is just not enough to say.

For the times I felt all hope was gone,
But you told me that I must hold on,
And you sent sunshine through clouds of gray,
"Thank you" is just not enough to say.

For answers to prayers you always send
And relationships you help to mend
And all of my debts you died to pay,
"Thank you" is just not enough to say.

1 THESSALONIANS 5: 16

*Be joyful always; pray continually; give thanks in all
circumstances, for this is God's will for you in Christ Jesus.*

ALONE WITH GOD

I must have this quiet time to spend with God alone;
I hunger for my Savior who claims me for His own.
It is a quest I can't deny---I search for His peace;
I bow before His throne so all earthly cares will cease.
I don't have to be in church kneeling at the altar
To speak to Him and ask for strength lest I should falter.
Any place is sacred when there's just the two of us
Away from all distractions and all the earthly fuss.
Satan sets up roadblocks to keep me from the Master;
He says we have no time; we must keep going faster.
But Satan's power cannot match my inner Spirit's will;
I have so deep a thirst that only my Lord can fill.
For there are things we must discuss, just between us two.
This is my true worship time, and nothing less will do.

JOHN 4:23

*Yet a time is coming and has now come when the true
worshipers will worship the Father in spirit and truth,
for they are the kind of worshipers the Father seeks.*

NO MORE ME

Lord, help me remove the "I"
And help me remove the "me."
Please allow "my will" to die;
Lord, just fill me up with "Thee."

From "myself," Lord, set me free
In each thing I say and do.
What I really want to be
Is completely filled with "You."

As I travel through this life
Meeting people face to face,
Please don't let them see my strife;
Let them only see "Your Grace."

JEREMIAH 9:23-24

This is what the Lord says: "Let not the wise man boast of his wisdom or the strong man boast of his strength or the rich man boast of his riches, but let him who boasts boast about this: that he understands and knows me, that I am the Lord, who exercises kindness, justice and righteousness on earth, for in these I delight," declares the Lord.

Please Let Me Stay With You

Father, I just want to sit here all day
And hear everything that you have to say.
I don't want to go out and face
Life's constant rat race.

Father, why can't I just sit here and pray---
Give you my burdens to carry away?
I need one sweet, calm day of rest.
This is my request.

Father, I know I have my bills to pay,
And work helps to keep collectors at bay;
But now I just need peace of mind---
Not the daily grind.

Father, each time, though I want to delay,
This world makes demands, and I cannot stay.
May I put it out of my mind
And just stay behind?

MARK 1:35-37

*Very early in the morning, while it was still dark, Jesus got up,
left the house and went off to a solitary place, where he prayed.
Simon and his companions went to look for him, and when they
found him, they exclaimed: "Everyone is looking for you!"*

Religion is not a relationship.

Everything belongs to God.

Love is the key.

Ask God for guidance.

Trust His Word and the Spirit.

I must deny my will.

Obedience is important.

Nothing else satisfies my soul.

Surrender all.

His will be done.

Identify with Christ.

Personally know God.

PHILIPPIANS 3:10

*I want to know Christ and the power of his resurrection and the
fellowship of sharing in his sufferings becoming like him in his death,
and so, somehow, to attain to the resurrection from the dead.*

FAITH

Matthew 17:20(b)

"I tell you the truth, if you have faith as small as a mustard seed, you can say to this mountain, 'Move from here to there' and it will move. Nothing will be impossible for you."

Hebrew 11:1

Now faith is being sure of what we hope for and certain of what we do not see.

SO THAT YOU MAY KNOW

Sometimes you wonder if God hears your cry,
Or if He's too busy to hear your sigh.
It seems that your pleas to Him pass on by,
And He doesn't care if you live or die;
But He sent His promise to you long ago
So that you may know.

The pathway is hard; there seems no way through;
You wonder still if God's listening to you.
You're hurting and lost and haven't a clue.
Life's got you down; you don't know what to do,
But He sent His Word to you long ago
So that you may know.

He once healed the blind and opened their eyes,
And lepers were cleansed to the people's surprise.
Demons were cast into pigs in their sties,
And even the dead He told to "Arise!"
But He sent His miracles long ago
So that you may know.

You think to yourself, "Why all this delay?"
Why doesn't He see you need it today?
He works all things out in His special way;
He hears every word when you kneel and pray,
But He sent His Son to earth long ago
So that you may know.

MATTHEW 9:1-8

*(v.4) Knowing their thoughts, Jesus said, "Why do you entertain
evil thoughts in your hearts? (v.5) Which is easier: to say, 'Your
sins are forgiven,' or to say, 'Get up and walk'? (v. 6) But so that
you may know that the Son of Man has authority on earth to
forgive sins…" Then he said to the paralytic, "Get up, take your
mat and go home." (v. 7) And the man got up and went home.*

MY FIRST LOVE

The day I accepted my salvation
I wanted to shout to every nation,
"See what the Lord has done for me!"
I would praise God's name everywhere I went
And work for Him until my strength was spent.
I was changed and wanted all to see.

Doing God's work was my great desire;
The Holy Spirit filled me with fire.
Nothing ever could stand in my way.
I wouldn't miss a chance to testify;
I would praise His name until the day I die.
I forgot that I have feet of clay.

For God's Word I had a mighty thirst;
When the church bells rang, I would get there first.
I even had my own special seat.
I volunteered for nearly everything;
I would pray, I would speak, and I would sing.
Serving God was now a special treat.

In time my resolve to go the distance
Began to meet with this world's resistance.
Sometimes, when church bells rang, I would be late.
Some days my Bible would go unread,
And perhaps my prayers would go unsaid,
And some good deeds would just have to wait.

My enthusiasm began to drop,
And the plans I made came to a stop.
I missed the joy I had when faith was new.
God gives us His warning from up above
That we should never lose our first love,
So I began to change my point of view.

It took will power and a lot of prayer,
But the Holy Spirit did get me there...
Back to the place where it all began,
Back to the foot of the old rugged cross
Where Satan suffered his greatest loss,
Back to my first love of salvation's plan.

REVELATION 2:4-5

*Yet I hold this against you: You have forsaken your first love.
Remember the height from which you have fallen! Repent
and do the things you did at first. If you do not repent, I will
come to you and remove your lampstand from its place.*

Down Through the Roof

When I'm paralyzed with fear
And don't know what to do,
It's good to know friends are near
To carry me on through.
They carry me to Jesus
With tears and bended knees,
For He's the One who frees us
And hears our earnest pleas.
It does not matter to them
What rooftop they must climb.
They set me right before Him
With prayers time after time.
Though often I may falter,
Our strengths we can combine.
They take me to the altar
And join their faith with mine.
Where two or three assemble
And are of one accord,
The devil starts to tremble
As we call on our Lord.
So when I feel I'm too weak
To reach Him on my own,
Through the prayers that my friends speak,
They place me at the throne.

Luke 5:17-26

Jesus Heals a Paralyzed Man (down through the roof).

Matthew 18:19-20

Again, I tell you that if two of you on earth agree about anything you ask for, it will be done for you by my Father in heaven. For where two or three come together in my name, there am I with them.

MY RED SEA

Lord, I do not know what Red Sea I may have to cross today---
What obstacles old Satan may see fit to put in my way.
The pathway could be treacherous, and the waters may run deep;
But you promised to protect me, and your promises you keep.

By day you are my cloud of shade, and by night you are my light;
And you'll hold back the waters and lead me safely through each plight.
So as I walk on dry land throughout my journey on this day,
I'll be secure in your care, with my enemies swept away.

EXODUS 13: 21

*By day the Lord went ahead of them in a pillar of cloud to
guide them on their way and by night in a pillar of fire to
give them light, so that they could travel by day or night.*

EXODUS 14: 21-22

*...The waters were divided, and the Israelites
went through the sea on dry ground.*

EXODUS 14: 29

*But the Israelites went through the sea on dry ground,
with a wall of water on their right and on their left.*

WALKING ON WATER

Lord, help me find the courage to step out of the boat;
And help me not to doubt, Lord, you will keep me afloat.
As you walked on water, an example for us all,
Let me be assured that you will catch me if I fall.
Don't let me fear that Satan will grasp me in his clutch,
For he will sink below as I reach out for your touch.
The waters may be dark and deep, and I know they're cold.
Create in me a spirit that is both brave and bold.
I need not fear the sordid things that this world can do.
I won't look at the water; I'll keep my eyes on you.

MATTHEW 14:22-31

*Immediately Jesus made the disciples get into the boat and go on ahead
of him to the other side, while he dismissed the crowd. After he had
dismissed them, he went up on a mountainside by himself to pray.
When evening came, he was there alone, but the boat was already a
considerable distance from land, buffeted by the waves because the
wind was against it. During the fourth watch of the night Jesus went
out to them, walking on the lake. When the disciples saw him walking
on the lake, they were terrified. "It's a ghost," they said, and cried
out in fear. But Jesus immediately said to them: "Take courage! It
is I. Don't be afraid." "Lord, if it's you," Peter replied, "tell me to
come to you on the water." "Come," he said. Then Peter got down
out of the boat, walked on the water and came toward Jesus. But
when he saw the wind, he was afraid and, beginning to sink, cried
out. "Lord, save me!" Immediately Jesus reached out his hand and
caught him. "You of little faith," he said, "why did you doubt?"*

FAITH IN THE FURNACE

Father, I have such a strong desire
For the faith to withstand any fire---
No matter how hot the flames may be
To know that you're standing here with me.

Faith in the furnace I long to know,
Like Shadrach, Meshach, Abednego.
From worldly flames I don't have to cringe;
I can walk through fire without a singe.

The fire has no power of its own,
But fueled by fear it's grown and grown.
The devil wants us to be afraid
And forget the price that Jesus paid.

Our fires may come in different ways,
But all around we can feel the blaze.
We each endure many trials by fire
From day of birth 'til funeral pyre.

God has promised we will not be burned,
For Satan's power Christ's blood has spurned.
So as fires rage above my head,
I'll put my trust in what God has said.

DANIEL 3: 17

*If we are thrown into the blazing furnace, the God we
serve is able to save us from it, and he will rescue us...*

DANIEL 3: 27

*...They saw that the fire had not harmed their bodies,
nor was a hair of their heads singed; their robes were not
scorched, and there was no smell of fire on them.*

A BLESSING IN DISGUISE

Lord, disappointment came by today
And tried to steal all my joy away.
Where once I was "up," now I am "down."
I had a smile but now wear a frown.
I had a plan, a hope, and a dream;
It was all laid out---a perfect scheme.
But things did not go as I had planned;
Life would not listen to my demand.
At first I searched for someone to blame
As I checked down my list name by name.
But in this life whatever we choose,
Sometimes we win, and sometimes we lose.
Each teaches a lesson we must learn---
Strong character traits that we must earn.
Sometimes it's so hard to recognize
When God sends a blessing in disguise.

PSALM 34:17-18

*The righteous cry out, and the Lord hears them; he delivers
them from all their troubles. The Lord is close to the
brokenhearted and saves those who are crushed in spirit.*

TEARS ON THE TABLE

We gather 'round the table to share each heavy load.
Alone we're just not able to travel life's hard road.
Though someone may never know his name is mentioned here,
From our hearts a prayer does flow because he is held dear
By someone at this table who loves him very much
And knows that God is able to heal him with a touch.
Each one takes a turn at prayer beseeching God above
That He'll send His special care to those we dearly love.
From broken hearts our tears flow; God gathers every one.
Each tear's a seed that we sow because God's precious Son
Made a way from this world's sod to Heaven's golden throne.
We can bow before our God and know we're not alone.
I'm thankful for every tear that trickles down each face
To this table as we're here with our sweet God of grace.

Job 16:20-21

My intercessor is my friend as my eyes pour out tears to God;
on behalf of a man he pleads with God as a man pleads for his friend.

SISTERS IN CHRIST

I guess that in reality our group seems very small.
It might be hard for some to see what good we do at all.
But we have things we bring to Him and place before His throne
When troubles come---so dark and grim---we can't face them alone.
When our world seems to fall apart and just keeps getting colder,
We give to Him each broken heart and cry upon His shoulder.
We are a band of sisters dear; we know when hearts are broken.
Some speak while others really hear words that are unspoken.
We share our grief and share our pain and sometimes share our tears.
When sorrows come like drops of rain, our sisterhood appears.
For Christ has made us "kin-folks" to fight despair and gloom;
To ward off Satan's "sin-yokes" while gathered in our room.
We join hearts around the table and go to God in prayer,
For we know our Lord is able; He's always waiting there.
We pray for family and friends and ones we do not know.
We pray that we might make amends with those who hurt us so.
We pray for all those in our church---'specially for our pastor;
And those who join us in our search for lost souls for our Master.
We ask our Lord to bless and keep leaders of our nation;
To give them wisdom fathoms deep in every situation.
We pray for mercy and for grace---that we will not stumble.
We pray for strength to run the race---not to trip and tumble
Into the great deceiver's sway as he with patience waits.
He wants to keep us far away from our dear Savior's gates.
We give God praise and thank Him, too, for love beyond compare;
For hard times He has helped us through; for this sweet hour we share.

MATTHEW 18:20

*For where two or three come together in my
name, there am I with them.*

36

PRAY WITHOUT CEASING

I often fall asleep at night while saying my prayers
As I carry to my Father my burdens and cares.
There are always many people I try to recall,
For they need a touch from Jesus, lest they slip and fall.
So many souls are suffering through illness and pain,
And many have lost loved ones as their tears fall like rain.
Disasters strike throughout the land, scattered far and wide.
I also pray I'll overcome any trace of pride.
I have so much to share with God and praises to give;
I could pray without ceasing for as long as I live.
So as I fall asleep at night, anxieties cease,
And I rest in the arms of God surrounded with peace.

1 Thessalonians 5:16-18

*Rejoice always, pray without ceasing, in everything give thanks;
for this is the will of God in Christ Jesus for you. (NKJV)*

PETER'S ESCAPE
Acts 12:1-17

King Herod chose to punish some members of God's church.
They captured some apostles as they began their search.
Dear James, who was John's brother, was murdered with a sword.
Then Peter soon was captured by Herod's evil horde,
And four full squads of soldiers with four in every squad
Were keeping strict surveillance to guard this man of God.
King Herod had intentions of putting him on trial.
Until Passover ended, he'd stay in jail a while.
The church was praying for him with earnest sincere prayer.
They begged God to save Peter and get him out of there.
The night before his trial, as Peter fell asleep,
Two soldiers sat beside him, so sure their watch to keep.
Both Peter's wrists were shackled with two chains strong and tight.
Sentries stood outside the door to guard him through the night.
Then suddenly an angel of the Lord did appear;
The dark cell was illumined with light so bright and clear.
The angel then struck Peter suddenly on his side.
"Quick, get up!" the angel said, as Peter's eyes grew wide.
The chains fell off Peter's wrists, and then the angel said,
"Put on your clothes and sandals." He did as he was led.
"Now wrap your cloak around you and follow after me."
Peter did as he was told, and soon he would be free.
Peter did not realize that all of this was real.
He thought it was a vision brought on by his ordeal.
They walked right past two sentries and reached the iron gate
That led into the city where Peter's people wait.
The gate opened by itself, and then they walked on through.
They walked the length of one street, an angel and a Jew.
Suddenly the angel left, and Peter then could see,
"Now I know without a doubt that God has rescued me."
He went to find his people where John Mark's mother dwelt.

They all were praying for him, as on their knees they knelt.
When Peter knocked on the door, a girl named Rhoda came.
She recognized Peter's voice and started to exclaim,
"Peter is outside the door!" For he still stood outside;
But no one there believed her. Her news they all denied.

When she kept on insisting that what she said was true,
They thought it was his angel. Now what were they to do?
As Peter kept on knocking, they peered outside with care,
And they were all astonished to see him standing there.
Then Peter motioned for them to pause so he could tell
How God had sent an angel to get him out of jail.
"Tell James and all the brothers what God has done today."
Thus Peter gave instructions and then went on his way.
Why were they so astonished with Peter safe and free?
Were they not praying for him right there on bended knee?
Are we not like those Christians who stood there clearly dazed?
When our God answers our prayers, why are we so amazed?

CRY TO THE ROCK

Why wait until His judgment day to seek a place to hide?
Why crouch down in a damp, dark cave because of willful pride?
It won't matter if we do have riches here on earth,
For that's not how our Father determines a soul's worth.
Wasted time will be tallied up…things we did and did not do,
And there is no place on this earth where His eyes can't see you.
When this world's days have come and gone, we all will realize
That hiding in our Savior's love is the only choice that's wise.
Those who refuse the Savior's gift of mercy and salvation
Will be vainly seeking refuge throughout every nation.
The rich and poor, the strong and weak, the highest and the low
Will scatter through fields and mountains but find nowhere to go.
They will plead for grace and mercy, but discover it's too late.
They will ask themselves the question, "Why, oh why, did I wait?"
Why wait and cry out to the rocks to cover sinful wages
When our sins could be washed away by the Rock of Ages?

REVELATION 6:15-17

*And the kings of the earth, the great men, the rich men, the
commanders, the mighty men, every slave and every free man, hid
themselves in the caves and in the rocks of the mountains, and said
to the mountains and rocks, "Fall on us and hide us from the face
of Him who sits on the throne and from the wrath of the Lamb! For
the great day of His wrath has come, and who is able to stand?"*

Sunlight and Shadows

Life is filled with sunlight and shadows. We hop, skip, and jump through the sunlit days, often feeling as if we are on top of the world and in complete control of our lives. Rest assured, however, that the shadows always appear---often when least expected.

God has His own ways of reminding us that He is indeed the One in control. When our backs are against the wall with nowhere else to turn, we are reminded that seeking Him is what we should have been doing all along. Because He loves us so very much, He will not let us get by for long thinking that we can make it on our own. Sometimes He sends gentle reminders of His place in our lives; other times they are not so gentle.

It is during the times of shadows that we truly grow. Just as some plants cannot grow when there is too much sunlight, we cannot. We must travel through the dark times as well as through the sunshine. It takes a variety of sunlight and shadows to form us into the people God intended for us to become. We can be certain, however, that, when the shadows seem to turn into total darkness in our lives, God is still beside us. He runs with us in the sunlight, He walks beside us in the shade, and He carries us through the darkness. It is only during all of these experiences that we can truly learn to trust Him.

"I trust God completely" is so easy to say, but it is not always so easy to live. Often we feel the need to have a "backup plan" just in case God does not fill our need when and how we think He should. As long as we need that backup plan, we are not completely trusting God. We should not have to be put into a position where we have "nowhere else to go but to Him" before we realize that He can always be trusted. I am thankful for the times He has put me in such positions, because it proves over and over again just how much He cares for me. He will not give up on teaching me to trust Him until I absolutely do, and He will not give up on you!

PROVERBS 3:5-6

Trust in the LORD with all your heart and lean not on your own understanding; in all your ways acknowledge him, and he will make your paths straight.

The Hem of His Garment

My life may, for a while, be as I think it should
With troubles left behind and everything all good;
When suddenly I'm crushed with trials I can't ignore,
I'm reaching for the hem of His garment once more.

I get back on my feet and think I will be strong
And start to feel secure that nothing can go wrong;
But as day turns to night and pain begins to pour,
I'm reaching for the hem of His garment once more.

When I begin to think I have life in control,
It's then that Satan starts a battle for my soul;
And just as I have done so many times before
I'm reaching for the hem of His garment once more.

So if I have to crawl down on my hands and knees
And push through crowds of grief to Him who saves and frees,
I'll reach the only One who heals each sinful sore
Each time I touch the hem of His garment once more.

MARK 5:24(B)-29

A large crowd followed and pressed around him. And a woman was there who had been subject to bleeding for twelve years. She had suffered a great deal under the care of many doctors and had spent all she had, yet instead of getting better she grew worse. When she heard about Jesus, she came up behind him in the crowd and touched his cloak, because she thought, "If I just touch his clothes, I will be healed." Immediately her bleeding stopped and she felt in her body that she was freed from her suffering.

ASSURANCE

Philippians 4:6-7

Do not be anxious about anything, but in
everything, by prayer and petition, with
thanksgiving, present your requests to God.
And the peace of God, which transcends
all understanding, will guard your hearts
and your minds in Christ Jesus.

EAGLE'S WINGS

Sometimes it seems my strength is spent
And I no longer have the will
To climb another steep ascent
To reach the top of one more hill.

My steps are slow; my breath is short;
I just cannot go the distance.
This task I feel I must abort,
For there's just too much resistance.

I sometimes feel I've hit the wall
And simply can't do one thing more,
As with each step I trip and fall
Until my body's bruised and sore.

When I reach the end of my rope
And feel my grasp begin to slip,
I turn to God, my source of hope,
And know He will renew my grip.

Though trials come that I must face
And I am plagued by worldly things,
With steady feet I'll run life's race,
And I will soar with eagle's wings.

ISAIAH 40:31

*But they that wait upon the Lord shall renew their strength;
they shall mount up with wings as eagles; they shall run,
and not be weary; and they shall walk, and not faint.*

FIRE AND FLOOD

The waters rushing toward me seemed so deep
It made me weep.
The waves from every side just battered me.
I tried to flee.
I slipped and felt that I was going down---
That I would drown;
But just as pain and sorrow neared my face,
I felt His grace.
He made a wall around me; it held back
Satan's attack.
Then fires came into my life instead.
I bowed my head.
They raged---surrounding me on every side.
My heart just cried.
I thought for sure this time my fate was sealed,
Then God revealed
His presence in the flames engulfing me.
Now I could see
Through trial by fire and flood He was my shield.
Oh, let me yield
My soul, my life, my heart, my everything
Unto my King.

ISAIAH 43:2; 4

*"When you pass through the waters, I will be with you; and
when you pass through the rivers, they will not sweep over
you. When you walk through the fire, you will not be burned;
the flames will not set you ablaze....Since you are precious
and honored in my sight, and because I love you,..."*

POWER FROM ABOVE

When God blew life into me,
There was no timidity.
"Boldly go; don't walk in fear,"
My Lord whispers in my ear.
"Don't hide and do not cower;
You are filled with my power.
Through me you have been made strong.
Stand firm, though the battle's long."

God has filled us with His love
With His spirit from above.
Love God and love your brother;
Give help to one another.
Train your heart and train your mind.
Leave your selfishness behind.
Discipline yourself to be
What He wants the world to see.

2 TIMOTHY 1:7

*For God did not give us a spirit of timidity, but a
spirit of power, of love and of self-discipline.*

AM I NOT STILL GOD?

Am I not still God when things go wrong,
When days are too hard and nights too long?
Am I not still God when your heart breaks,
When your mind is tired; your body aches?
Am I not still God when skies are gray,
When rain clouds wash all your dreams away?
Am I not still God when all seems lost,
When you beg for peace at any cost?
Am I not still God when your loved one
Reaches the end of life's race he's run?
Am I not still God when illness falls,
When war is declared and duty calls?
Am I not still God when trouble's near,
When all your friends seem to disappear?
Am I not still God when wrong seems right,
When you lose your job and money's tight?
Am I not still God when nerves are frayed,
When your good intentions seem outweighed?
Am I not still God when children stray,
When all hope seems to have gone away?
Am I not still God when you may doubt,
When Satan attacks---day in---day out?
Am I not still God, the great I Am,
Your Lord and Savior, God's chosen Lamb?

EXODUS 3:14

*God said to Moses, "I AM WHO I AM. This is what you
are to say to the Israelites: 'I AM has sent me to you.'"*

CONSISTENCY

This world is always changing;
My life keeps rearranging;
I try to slow it down without success.
It seems I'm always racing
Or nervously I'm pacing
And getting more behind, I must confess.

I find little time to pause.
I am stressed out just because
I seem to put my cart before my horse.
The winds of change keep blowing;
Against the tide I'm rowing,
And then I wonder how I got off course.

I know that I'm not able
To keep life sane and stable;
I need one thing on which I can depend.
Through present, past, tomorrow;
Through happiness and sorrow;
Christ will not change, though earthly things shall end.

HEBREWS 13: 8

Jesus Christ is the same yesterday and today and forever.

FEAR NOT

It's easy to say, "Have no fear,"
When there's no danger near.
With ease we wear a smile sublime
When there's no hill to climb.
With ease we say, "He is my Rock"
When there's no stumbling block.
With ease we say, "Have a nice day"
When all things go our way.

How easy, though, to face this life
When it is filled with strife?
How easy is it just to stand
When life gets out of hand?
To watch a loved one accept death
And take that final breath?
How easy is it not to fear
When Satan's lurking here?

"Do not fear, for I am with you,"
God tells us, and it's true.
"Be not dismayed," is His command,
"For you are in my hand.
This life can be so very hard
You'll get both bruised and scarred;
But when you feel you're at a loss,
Keep looking at my cross."

ISAIAH 41:10

*Fear not, for I am with you. Be not dismayed, for I
am your God. I will strengthen you and help you. I
will uphold you with my righteous right hand.*

SECURITY

Lord, when I don't know what to do,
It seems I always cling to you.
When it appears all hope is gone,
I reach for you and just hold on.

When I am overcome with fear,
I hear you whisper that you're near;
And just before I sink below,
I grab your hand and won't let go.

When my whole world turns inside out,
And Satan tries to make me doubt,
And I'm not certain how I feel,
Your arms just hold me closer still.

Lord, in my fragile human form,
I often pass through life's dark storm.
You are the right that fights the wrong.
I know I'm weak, but you are strong.

I cannot move one single step
Without you by my side to help.
I'll cling to you 'til my last breath,
And in your arms I'll lie in death.

PSALM 16:8

*I have set the Lord always before me. Because He
is at my right hand, I will not be shaken.*

OUR REFUGE

The Lord said, "Child, as you walk through this dark place
It may seem that you cannot see my face
Or hear my voice or feel my loving grace,
But have no fear, for you're in my embrace."

The Lord said, "Child, this trouble is severe;
Your strife and pain all seem so very near.
You call my name and wonder if I hear.
I love you, Child, and my word is sincere."

The Lord said, "Child, the hill might seem too high,
And you can't see why you should even try.
You hear the mob as they shout, 'Crucify!'
But have no fear, my grace reaches the sky."

The Lord said, "Child, I know the river's wide;
You feel your life's been pounded by the tide.
Your instinct screams, 'Just run away and hide!'
But have no fear, for I am by your side."

The Lord said, "Child, I made the earth and sea;
For all your needs, look to the Trinity.
You know I died that you could be set free,
And where you are, that is where I will be."

PSALM 46:1-2

God is our refuge and strength, an ever-present help in trouble. Therefore we will not fear, though the earth give way and the mountains fall in the heart of the sea,...

MY HERO

There may be those who would face death and give up life for me,
But only one could save my soul and set my spirit free.
There's only one who loves me beyond any measure;
Only one who thinks of me as a priceless treasure;
One who takes delight in me; renews me with his love;
Leads the Heavenly choir with singing from above;
Rejoices over me as though I'm His only one;
Instills in me the Spirit of His own begotten Son.

ZEPHANIAH 3:17

*The Lord your God is with you, he is mighty to save.
He will take great delight in you, he will quiet you with
his love, he will rejoice over you with singing.*

CONFUSION

I tried to do it my way;
It was a mess.
Again I tried it my way
Without success.

I tried to speak with my words;
They made no sense.
Again I spoke with my words;
They caused offense.

I tried to think just good thoughts,
But bad slipped in.
I sought so hard for good thoughts
My head would spin.

I thought I was all grown-up---
Was in control.
But each and every grown-up
Must guard his soul.

Then God looked down at my life
And saw my plight.
When God looked down at my life,
He joined the fight.

He showed me that old Satan
Was standing there.
He showed me that old Satan
Was everywhere.

He told me, "Child, you'd better
Just let me guide."
He said, "My child, you'd better
Walk by my side.

We'll act and speak together,
Bone of my bone.
We'll act and speak together.
You're not alone."

---

2 Corinthians 12:9(a)

*But he said to me, "My grace is sufficient for you,
for my power is made perfect in weakness."*

He Just Keeps On Loving Us

Though many things I do not know, I know one thing for sure;
I know His love is faithful, and I know His heart is pure.
Though I fail Him time and again and cause His heart to grieve,
I know He will not let me down, and He will never leave.
The gift of free will He gave me; I have the right to choose.
With Him I am a winner; with the World I always lose.
So many things, while here on earth, I'll never understand;
But I know through all my troubles, I'm held up by His hand.
Even though we cause Him pain with the things we say and do,
He just keeps on loving me, and He keeps on loving you.

<><><><><><><><><><><><><><><><><><><><><><><><><><><><><><><><>

PSALM *9:10*

Those who know your name will trust in you, for you,
Lord, have never forsaken those who seek you.

<><><><><><><><><><><><><><><><><><><><><><><><><><><><><><><><>

The Apple of His Eye

There is a constant battle raging deep inside of us,
And it just gets much stronger 'neath our daily strife and fuss.

Sometimes we feel so all alone despair comes creeping in,
And everywhere we turn it seems we run into more sin.

Instead of words of hope, we hear the gossip and the lies.
By casting down a child of God, we just don't realize

That what we do to God's own child, we do to Him above.
It matters if we cast those stones or sow those seeds of love.

We must take care to feel the hurts and hear the whispered sigh,
For each of God's own children is the apple of His eye.

ZECHARIAH 2:8

"...for whoever touches you touches the apple of his eye."

NOT TODAY

I lived in dread of things to come,
Though I had no control.
My entire world seemed dark and glum;
No joy was in my soul.

Fear gnawed inside and made me ill;
It seemed I had no hope.
Life had become a bitter pill;
All I could do was mope.

When joy was gone, I had a choice,
To fight or just give in.
Then suddenly I heard God's voice;
He told me I could win.

"My child, when Satan's darts attack
With threats of death and doom,
Stand strong and fight! I've got your back,
Between us there's no room.

There may be things that you must face
When you can't run away,
But don't miss out on this day's grace!
Tell Satan, 'Not today!'"

1 Peter 5:8

Be self-controlled and alert. Your enemy the devil prowls around like a roaring lion looking for someone to devour.

MOUNTAINS AND CLOUDS

How often does a cloud hang low
And hide the mountaintop,
When that is where we need to go
To make our anguish stop?

How near we come to heights unknown
But stop before we're there.
We feel we're climbing all alone,
As we drown in despair.

When gazing from the valley deep,
There seems no way to climb
A mountain standing tall and steep;
It seems a waste of time.

But if we never traveled through
A valley deep and wide,
We might not learn to trust Him who
Waits on the other side.

Not only does God wait to greet
His children at the top,
He also guides our stumbling feet
And will not let us drop.

So though a cloud may hide the view
For just a little while,
We have a God who'll guide us through
Each long and painful mile.

PSALM 121:1

*I lift up my eyes to the hills---where does my help come from? My
help comes from the Lord, the Maker of heaven and earth.*

GOD IS LOVE

God loves me! Why can't I just know that and worry about nothing?
What if the Bible consisted of just three words: "God is Love"?
Shouldn't that be enough for us?
Why do we often think, "I know He loves me, **but** …"?

> **Yes, God loves me, this I know;**
> **So why do I worry so?**
> **Why do I think that I must**
> **Make my plans if Him I trust?**
> **Why can't I lie down in peace**
> **And let God my fears release?**

---

1 JOHN 4:10, 18

*This is love: not that we loved God, but that he loved us and sent
his Son as an atoning sacrifice for our sins. There is no fear in
love. But perfect love drives out fear, because fear has to do with
punishment. The one who fears is not made perfect in love.*

ABOUT MYSELF

Acts 20:24

However, I consider my life worth nothing to me, if only I may finish the race and complete the task the Lord Jesus has given me---the task of testifying to the gospel of God's grace.

IF I HAD KNOWN

If I had known how sweet this peace would be,
If I had known this feeling to be free,
If I had known the beauty I could see,
I would have knelt down sooner.

If I had known the mountains I could climb,
If I had known forgiveness so sublime,
If I had known the value of my time,
I would have knelt down sooner.

If I had known the Spirit I could feel,
If I had known the hurts that Christ could heal,
If I had known about my Father's will,
I would have knelt down sooner.

ROMANS 14:11

*It is written: " 'As surely as I live,' says the Lord, 'every knee
will bow before me; every tongue will confess to God.' "*

Look Up

It came to my mind one day as I was walking our dog and gazing *up* at the beautiful hills of West Virginia, where we were working at the time, that we find most of life's goodness and beauty while we are *"looking up."* It also dawned on me that, whenever we need to find information or direction, we *"look it up."* When we are fighting the battles of life, we **look up** for help and comfort. I think that it is not by accident that we use those words during those times.

When we seek God's direction for our lives, we **look upward**. When we praise His name, we lift our hands and voices **upward**. When we need His help, we **look upward**. In Psalm 121:1-2 we find the words "I will **lift up** mine eyes unto the hills, from whence cometh my help. My help cometh from the LORD, which made heaven and earth." (KJV)

Moses went **up** the mountain to talk to God. As Stephen was being stoned to death, he looked **up** at the glory of Heaven. At His ascension, Jesus lifted **up** His hands to bless the disciples and then He was taken **up** into heaven. Christ often went **up** on a mountain to pray to His Father. Elijah was taken **up** to heaven in a whirlwind.

God placed an innate desire inside each one of us to **look up**, to **rise up**, and to **reach up**. Often this world tries to squelch that natural tendency because Satan wants us to look down, to fall down, and to stay down. I guess a lot of life's choices boil down to this. Do we want to crawl low with Satan or soar **up** high with God? That seems to be an easy choice to make. Why then do so many people make the wrong one?

ACTS 7:55-56

*But Stephen, full of the Holy Spirit, **looked up to heaven**
and saw the glory of God, and Jesus standing at the right
hand of God. "Look," he said, "I see heaven open and the
Son of Man standing at the right hand of God."*

I WANT TO BE REACHING

Made in His image and formed in a womb,
Then sent to a distant place,
We start out in life and end in a tomb
Still seeking our Savior's face.

We are born reaching for an unseen hand
That we felt before our birth.
We sense a need we do not understand…
Christ linking Heaven to Earth.

When Christ reaches down and claims for his own
The saints truly beseeching,
He'll take us higher than we've ever known.
Lord, I want to be reaching!

PHILIPPIANS 3:12-14

*Not that I have already obtained all this, or have already been
made perfect, but I press on to take hold of that for which Christ
Jesus took hold of me. Brothers, I do not consider myself yet to have
taken hold of it. But one thing I do: Forgetting what is behind and
straining toward what is ahead, I press on toward the goal to win
the prize for which God has called me heavenward in Christ Jesus.*

GOD INSIDE

As I go on throughout this day
Greeting all those along my way,
I pray that everyone can see
That my Lord dwells inside of me.

Someone may need a smile from Him
Because his world seems dark and grim.
God may have sent me there today
To give that certain smile away.

Perhaps there is that one kind word
That from my lips just must be heard,
Or some good deed that should be done
To show God's love for that "someone."

I do not know whom He will send;
A stranger could become a friend.
For some are waiting just to see
The Christ who lives inside of me.

JOHN 13:34-35

"A new command I give you: Love one another. As I have loved you, so you must love one another. By this all men will know that you are my disciples, if you love one another."

LIFE'S ROAD

Lord, I'm tired of bearing this heavy load
As I travel down life's beautiful road.
My back grows weary; sometimes I stumble.
Then off in the distance, storm clouds rumble.
My Soul feels the forecast predicting pain.
My heartache is lightning; my tears are its rain.
I feel the lows of earthly depression
Amid downpours of heartfelt confession.
In floods of troubles I search for your boat---
That one called "Mercy" which keeps me afloat.
As waters get deeper down life's highway,
I look to Heaven for just one bright ray.
When I call your name, I'm rescued by you,
And suddenly sunshine comes shining through.
You are my Captain and you know life's course.
Your Son overcame this world's darkest force.
So even though I should tumble and toss,
I'll get safely through---my anchor's your cross.
As your loving hand guides me to the shore,
I find that I've lost that burden I bore.
You've taken control---assumed my full load.
With joy and great thanks, I'm traveling life's road.

Matthew 7: 25

The rain came down, the streams rose, and the winds
blew and beat against that house, yet it did not fall,
because it had its foundation on the rock.

HELP ME CLEAR THE PATH

When worldly things obscure my view,
Lord, show me what I need to do
To see the things I know are true,
And keep my eyes affixed on you.

When worldly things attack my mind
And crush me in the daily grind,
Lord, let me look to you and find
Your peace and put such thoughts behind.

When worldly things try to deplete
My strength and knock me off my feet
And Satan lures me with deceit,
Lord, keep me from the world's defeat.

When worldly things cause me to trip
And from your way I start to slip
And I am like a sinking ship,
Please hold me tightly in your grip.

When worldly things get in my way,
Life's road is filled with sin's decay,
And stumbling blocks cause me to stray,
Lord, help me clear the path each day.

Matthew 7:13

*Enter through the narrow gate, for wide is the gate and broad is
the road that leads to destruction, and many enter through it.*

Melancholy Mood

As I sit here alone and still
And not too certain how I feel,
I wait for God to speak to me
And seek His Word so desperately.

I listen for my Master's voice
To make my weary soul rejoice
And make this empty space within
Feel satisfied and full again.

Without a word from God each day
Before I go to work or play
I'm like a traveler with no map-
A grumpy child without a nap.

I can't get life to work out right;
I'm in the dark without a light.
I need His guidance and His grace
Before I run this world's hard race.

So I must take a moment now
To come before His throne and bow
And ask if He will be my guide
And stand forever by my side.

PSALM 31:3

*Since you are my rock and my fortress, for the
sake of your name lead and guide me.*

A FRIEND IN NEED

Lord, my heart is heavy today;
I have a friend who's in trouble.
I'm not quite sure just what to say;
You see, life has "burst her bubble."
To most it seems she does possess
All the worldly things we pursue;
But now her life is in a mess,
And she just needs some peace from you.
She loves you, Father, and your son,
And I know that her faith is strong.
She wonders now what she has done
To make the struggle last so long!
She's walking through the fire and flood,
And she is trying not to fear;
For she's protected by Christ's blood,
And Jesus feels her every tear.
I beg you, God, to give her peace;
Father, help her not to falter.
Please from this pain her soul release;
Let her place it on your altar.

GALATIANS 6:2

Bear ye one another's burdens, and so fulfill the law of Christ.

OUR WEAKEST PLACES

Never think for one moment that Satan does not know our weakest and most vulnerable places. He plays dirty and has no remorse about just how low he is willing to go to destroy what God has created. He knows how much God loves His children, and he knows how much most of us love ours. That gives him perfect targets in his quest to cause havoc in our lives.

Satan knows that, if he can destroy our families, he can take over more and more of this world. It has been proven throughout the ages that, when the families are strong, the country is strong. Unfortunately, it works both ways--- weak families create a weak country. Even though he loves to cause desolation in mass quantities, he is also in a state of elation with each individual soul he is able to snare.

Now that I think about it, "snare" is the perfect word for Satan's work. One definition of that word is "something by which one is entangled, involved in difficulties, or impeded." I suppose that is why we often hear that someone is "entangled" in a web of sin. A web is one of this world's strongest creations; and, once someone becomes entangled, it is nearly impossible for that person to free himself. Likewise, **it is impossible for any of us to free ourselves from the entanglement of sin.** Jesus Christ is the only One who can free any of us from such a web, and He offers to do so absolutely free of charge.

I love the words from **Isaiah 49:25** which give us this assurance: *"But this is what the LORD says: 'Yes, captives will be taken from warriors, and plunder retrieved from the fierce; I will contend with those who contend with you, <u>and your children I will save.</u>' "*

We must entrust our children to the care of God. By placing them into His hands, we are putting them in the safest possible place they can be. The waiting may be long, and their lives may not go the way we planned, but let us rest in His promise when He tells us, "Your children I will save."

MY SON

Lord, I have a son, too,
Though he's just a mortal man.
I love mine like you do,
And I've done the best I can.
Somewhere along life's way
He has taken a wrong turn.
He knows the price he'll pay,
But it seems he will not learn.
You said to raise him up
In the way that he should go
Then you would fill his cup;
With grace it would overflow.
I tried to teach him "right,"
But it seems he's chosen "wrong."
I know your hold is tight,
And I know your hold is strong.
You'll do what must be done
To bring my child back in line;
Because I love your son,
And I know that you love mine.

PROVERBS 22:6

*Train up a child in the way he should go; and when
he is old, he will not depart from it. (KJV)*

OUR CHILDREN

All too soon children are grown up and gone,
So independent with lives of their own.
Flowers in our garden, pruned through the years,
They're fed with our love---watered with our tears.
God's greatest blessing, they're sent from above
To teach us endurance, patience and love.
Through all their trials, it's our job to guide.
No matter what comes, we stand by their side.
We know they must leave us, and we know why;
Yet it is so hard to teach them to fly.
We send them out like arrows from a bow,
But in our hearts we will never let go.

PSALM 127:3-5

*Sons are a heritage from the Lord, children a reward from
him. Like arrows in the hands of a warrior are sons born in
one's youth. Blessed is the man whose quiver is full of them.*

1 KINGS 19:20

*..."Let me kiss my father and mother good-by," he
said, "and then I will come with you."*

GOD'S HANDS

When God looks into the palms of His hands,
He sees my name. I know He understands
What's in my heart and all my hurts and needs.
On my barren life He surely plants the seeds
Of fruit and manna on which my soul feeds.
He bears witness to all my earthly deeds.

He is so great, and I'm so very small.
Why should I matter to my Lord at all?
And yet He helps me through each trial and test;
He gives me strength to stand, then gives me rest.
The least I owe Him is my utmost best;
With His own blood He did in me invest.

That He should care I cannot comprehend,
But to each care and woe He does attend.
My <u>Bible</u> states that He knows me by name,
And there could be no higher claim to fame.
Because He lives, my soul can now proclaim,
"He is my God---I'll never be the same!"

ISAIAH 49:16

*See, I have engraved you on the palms of my
hands; your walls are ever before me.*

THE CLEANSING

I cleaned out some clutter today
And threw some old feelings away.
Regrets hung there all in a row
With guilt and blame piled up below.
Fear and confusion took much room
Along with pain, sadness and gloom.
Heartache was there taking up space.
I threw it out---left not one trace.
One whole shelf was filled with despair.
Bitterness was tossed everywhere.
One section was filled with tension;
So much stress---too much to mention!
Resentment I had shoved far back
I dragged out and tossed in a sack.
Envy and greed lay on one shelf;
Times I had thought just of myself.
Some things had been there far too long,
Even though I knew they were wrong.
Pride and shame were last to depart
As God helped me clean up my heart.

PSALM 51:10

*Create in me a pure heart, O God,
and renew a steadfast spirit within me.*

A NEW HEART

Lord, give me a light that shines for you.
Lord, give me a HEART that pines for you.
Lord, give me a mouth that speaks for you.
Lord, give me a HEART that seeks for you.
Lord, give me an ear that hears for you.
Lord, give me a HEART that fears for you.
Lord, give me a will that bends for you.
Lord, give me a HEART that mends for you.
Lord, give me a mind that learns for you.
Lord, give me a HEART that yearns for you.
Lord, give me a soul that longs for you.
Lord, give me a HEART with songs for you.
Lord, give me a hand that heals for you.
Lord, give me a HEART that feels for you.
Lord, give me a need that stays for you.
Lord, give me a HEART that prays for you.
Lord, give me a touch that cares for you.
Lord, give me a HEART that shares for you.

Lord, give me a HEART that's all brand new!

⟡⟡⟡

EZEKIEL 36:26-27

*I will give you a new heart and put a new spirit in you; I
will remove from you your heart of stone and give you a
heart of flesh. And I will put my Spirit in you and move you
to follow my decrees and be careful to keep my laws.*

⟡⟡⟡

MY BURDEN

Lord, how many times have I given to you
This very same burden and asked you to do
Something to lighten this great load that I bear?
I gave it to you, but did not leave it there.

My heart is so heavy for my loved one dear;
I've begged and I've pleaded, but he just won't hear.
I've prayed and I've had others pray for him, too.
I've asked for protection for his soul from you.

In my heart I am sure you'll take care of him
And be his bright beacon when life seems too dim.
I know that you hear, and I know that you care;
I gave this to you, but did not leave it there.

Then one day as we just sat talking in prayer,
You took this great burden I'd chosen to bear.
You lifted it up like a physical weight,
And took it with you right through Heaven's bright gate.

That burden I'd carried, now I could release
And replace it with joy, contentment, and peace.
It's out of my hands and now all in your care;
It's laid at your feet, and I'm leaving it there.

PSALM 81:6

He says, "I removed the burden from their shoulders;..."

GOD'S TROPHY ROOM

If life is a contest with my soul as a prize
Between God with His grace and Satan in disguise,
Then as my lifetime on Earth so rapidly flies,
I must build on the Rock like the man who was wise.

For to win such a contest, the devil will cheat.
It would be his delight if our Lord he'd defeat;
But no matter how high Satan turns up the heat,
He knows God is the victor each time that they meet.

So he works through us mortals---he knows we are weak.
He calls us names like "Holy Joe" or "Jesus Freak."
But Christ says the blessed include those who are meek
Just as long as His image is all that we seek.

The battle has raged since we were born from the womb
With Satan's ammunition of despair and gloom;
But our Lord overcame when He rose from the tomb,
And He made a place for us in God's trophy room.

MATTHEW 7: 24

*"Therefore everyone who hears these words of mine and puts them
into practice is like a wise man who built his house on the rock."*

MATTHEW 5: 5

"Blessed are the meek, for they shall inherit the earth."

Something I Learned From Mama

Growing up was hard back in the nineteen twenties and thirties, especially for a shy little girl from a poor family. As soon as she was old enough, she plodded along between long rows of cotton while filling her sack with fluffy white bolls. The cotton hulls often nicked her tiny hands, and by dark they were sore and often bleeding. She was the second of five surviving children, and each one had to pull his or her weight.

Although times were very lean, she never once had to go hungry. A meal might consist of a cold biscuit with maybe a dollop of syrup, but she did not have to go to bed with a noisy stomach; therefore, she considered herself to be very blessed.

On Christmas morning she was thankful for the orange, nuts, and hard candy that she found in her stocking. She remembers one special Christmas when she found a little red purse that was left for her under the tree. What an unforgettable treasure that was!

Times were much simpler then, and many years have passed since that wonderful Christmas morning. Now she could have all of the purses she might desire, but none could compare to that little red one. Her children and grandchildren will probably never understand that feeling she experienced on that long ago Christmas morning, and that is really a shame. We all need to learn that an abundance of "things" can never make us happy---they just give us more about which to worry.

Our country is now in very bad shape, and it is time to return to the simple things in life. We should be thankful every day if we have food in our stomachs, clothes on our bodies, and a warm, safe place to reside. Many people do not have these very basic things. Let us never cease to be thankful for the simple things of life. Try to recall the "little red purse" in your life.

PSALM 75:1

*We give thanks to you, O God, we give thanks, for your
Name is near; men tell of your wonderful deeds.*

CHANGES

I did not understand your plan;
I did not want to go that way.
The gulf that you asked me to span
Revealed to me my feet of clay.

Though I recoiled with fear and doubt
And tried in vain to turn and run,
I soon found there was no way out,
And your new plan had just begun.

I sought your will with prayers and tears;
I searched Your Word as if starving.
Where would it lead, through what strange spheres,
This path for me you were carving?

At last I knew I had no choice;
I had to leave my comfort zone.
I'll admit I did not rejoice.
Yet, still I went. I felt alone.

I ventured out on a new quest
With unsure steps and heavy heart---
Not sure if I could pass this test,
But knowing it was time to start.

You asked me to give up a life
That was all I had ever known.
My security had turned to strife,
And all my peace of mind was gone.

Then suddenly you spoke to me,
And your voice could not be denied.
My peace returned, for I could see
To all my questions you replied,

"Child, someone out there needs to hear
What I have given you to share;
And though I send you far or near,
You can trust that I will be there."

PSALM 4:8

I will lie down and sleep in peace, for you alone,
O LORD, make me dwell in safety.

The "P" Word

Most people have heard about the "C" word, but shortly before my fifth birthday in 1953 my family and I learned about the "P" word. I was diagnosed with polio.

After a visit to the office of our family physician, my parents were told what he suspected. I was taken to a nearby hospital where a pediatrician confirmed their worst fears. While at that hospital, I became paralyzed from the neck down. I can only imagine how my parents must have felt when I told them, "I can't move anything but my head." Of course, I did not realize the full impact of those words.

The pediatrician was a very good doctor, and he administered some kind of polio vaccine even though I already had the disease. As he told my parents, "It can't hurt." Indeed, it did not hurt. It possibly kept me from being permanently paralyzed…that and the Lord.

I remember being transported that very night to a "polio center" over one hundred miles away. To the best of my memory, I was placed in the back seat of my parents' car, and Daddy drove while Mama worried. Actually, I am certain they were both worried. Even though it was against the rules, the nurses let Mama stay with me for the remainder of that night. From that time on, for the next three weeks, there were strict visiting hours.

I saw many things while I was there. Even though I was very young, I can remember a lot of it. There were six of us children in one area of the large, open, community-type room. Our group consisted of three girls and three boys. I wish I could know how the others turned out and where they are today. We became very close during that three-week confinement. We all went through rigid routines of physical therapy, but the workers tried to make it as much fun as possible. Mama and I went through those same exercises for a full year after I went home. I remember being so happy when that last day of exercise was over. Now I wish I had kept them up for all of the following years. I would be in much better shape now, if I had!

We met people who lived in "iron lungs" in order to be able to breathe. Many of them were young. One young man had been recently married, and I remember his wife sitting there day after day. The only part of him that was visible outside the iron lung was his head, and that was how he spent the rest of his days in this life. I don't think he lived very many more years. There were many cases like his.

That brings me to my point in writing this. Why did I recover with nothing to show for that experience except a small dent in a muscle in my right arm? There is nothing wrong with the muscle; it is still strong and never bothers me. I seldom think about any of this, but I need to remember. God has a plan for my life. He has left me here for quite a while. I pray that I have not been too much of a disappointment to Him. To me, the "P" word is not "polio." The "P" word is "praise."

PSALM 146:2

*I will praise the LORD all my life; I will sing
praise to my God as long as I live.*

The "C" Word

In 1986 I heard a doctor use the word "malignant" when discussing a biopsy he had just performed on me. I do not know how to describe the immediate feeling that accompanied that conversation. It really was not a feeling of fear or disbelief or even of surprise. I had known the possible outcome. My mother had heard that same word in reference to herself about eight years before, and she was still with me at the hospital that day. She and my husband had already been told what the biopsy showed, and they were trying to be nonchalant until the doctor arrived to talk to me. They were not very good actors. Fortunately for them, the doctor walked in quickly and told me the news. "We'll have to do something," he said. "Yes," I replied, "we'll have to do something."

The following day I was taken to a very cold, sterile room decorated with signs containing the words "nuclear medicine." I was to have a bone scan, and that involved injecting me with some of that nuclear medicine. It is not a very comforting feeling when the person administering your medication has to hide behind a lead vest and a protective screen during the procedure. To make matters worse, I was left alone in that huge room while the medicine worked its way throughout my body and into my bones.

It was at that particular moment that everything involved in this new adventure of my life began to really hit home. Fear began to creep inside my mind. Even though I had much support from family and friends, loneliness was the only companion I could feel during those moments. What was there to do? Pray!!! No sooner had I started to pray than I felt a presence sitting beside me on that cold, hard, metal examination table. It was not a presence that I could see, but it was as real to me as that table. I don't know if it was an angel or Christ himself, but someone sat there on my right side and placed an arm around my shoulders. The coldness of the room was replaced by warmth from that presence. The fear disappeared. I was not alone. I was loved and comforted. That moment changed a lot in my life. I had been brought up to know that God does exist, and I had always believed that fact. Then, however, I KNEW!!! I really KNEW!!! Whatever the outcome of this experience was to be, there was nothing to fear. I was actually in a "win-win" situation.

I still do not understand why God chose me to remain here while others were chosen to leave this world, carried away by that same disease. I know there were things on earth that He must have wanted me to do, and I pray that I have done those things to His satisfaction and will continue to do as long as I am in this world. It is my desire to serve Him while I am here and to live with Him for eternity when I leave. There are days when I feel weak and other days when I feel strong. I must guard against both kinds of days. I must never forget His power and never overestimate my own. Apart from Him, I have no power.

"Cancer" is an intimidating word. It is a disease that attacks not only the body but also the spirit. I am so thankful that we have a Spirit that is stronger than cancer. God's Spirit is able to carry us through those times in our lives when there seems to be no way through. I no longer associate the "C" word with "cancer." I now associate it with "Christ."

PSALM 142:1-3(A)

*I cry aloud to the LORD; I lift up my voice to the
LORD for mercy. I pour out my complaint before him;
before him I tell my trouble. When my spirit grows
faint within me, it is you who know my way.*

JEREMIAH 29:11

Lord, I'm nearly five, and so far from grown.
There hasn't been any hardship I've known,
But this morning I woke up not feeling well.
My parents were worried; I could just tell.
The doctor said something is terribly wrong;
I needed special help, and don't take too long.
"Polio" is what he mentioned to us,
Though I don't understand about all the fuss.
As Mama laid me on the hospital bed,
Suddenly all I could move was my head.
I don't understand about "paralyze."
I guess I'm too young; I'm just not that wise.
I wasn't afraid---just simply amazed,
Not knowing the threat to the rest of my days.
God, my mama and daddy were crying.
They acted as if they thought I was dying.
Father, I really just don't understand.
They've taught me to rest in the palm of your hand.
But, I am their daughter, and they're full of fear.
Remind them, dear Lord, that you're always near.
Lord, thank you for doctors who help us to heal.
Thank you for giving them that kind of skill.
I still wonder why you chose me to be
Cured of an illness that could have killed me.
There is never enough that I can do.
Lord, let my life make a difference for you.

Lord, the years of my life are now thirty-eight;
This year has been hard like some heavy weight.
My family has faced many ordeals
So we'll understand how someone else feels

And perhaps help some others make it through
When they're lost in the dark and don't know what to do.
Once again a doctor gave me bad news;
"Malignant" is the word he chose to use.
I can't say I was really too surprised,
Though Mike and Mama had tried to disguise
The fear they felt because of their love for me.
Their eyes revealed what they hoped I wouldn't see.
Amid all the round of medical tests,
I tried to be strong, Lord, I did my best;
But suddenly in a room all alone,
I began to feel that all hope was gone.
In that lowest moment with nowhere to hide,
I felt you, Jesus, right there by my side.
Your arms slipped around me. You said, "I am here."
Then your sweet, sweet peace replaced all my fear.
I knew that it all would turn out just right,
For Jesus, my Savior, had joined in the fight.
I still wonder, God, why you chose me to be
Cured of an illness that could have killed me.
There is never enough that I can do.
Lord, let my life make a difference for you.

JEREMIAH 29:11

"For I know the plans I have for you," declares the Lord, "plans to prosper you and not to harm you, plans to give you hope and a future."

PLANS

I had plans to tell the world about my Lord and God.
I started mapping out the whole pathway I would trod.
I love my Lord and Savior, and many need to know.
I had plans to tell the world, but never did I go.

So I thought I'd share His Word with people in our land,
For many in our country just do not understand.
When Jesus said to "Go," I knew I was one He meant.
I had that journey planned, but somehow I never went.

Then I decided I should just witness in our state.
I knew that I must hurry, for time was growing late.
But even though I felt a great longing in my heart,
Time kept ticking onward, and I never did depart.

I thought, "Our community is really very small;
To tell them about Jesus would be no chore at all."
But although I often traveled back and forth to town,
The days kept slipping by, and I never "got around."

Now that I was older, I decided that I should
Witness to a person living in my neighborhood.
The Spirit often told me to stop and go inside,
But I thought, "I'll do that later." Then I heard she had died.

Still the Spirit beckoned, "Go speak to your family.
Tell them of their Savior and the Father and of Me.
Let them know we love them and want them to love us, too.
They can have the same salvation that we offered you."

So I rushed to my loved ones making sure they could see
Their souls can dwell with Jesus throughout eternity.
For from this world I must depart and leave some loved ones here,
But I can live forever with those I hold so dear.

When I think of all my plans to go and testify
And all the opportunities I let slip on by,
I will have no excuse as I stand before God's throne,
And He asks about the chances I had but are now gone.

I'm thankful that I still have time to go out and share
And tell about my Savior to people everywhere.
I never can reclaim all the times that slipped away,
But thank the Lord and praise His name; I still have "today."

MATTHEW 28:18-20(A)

*Then Jesus came to them and said, "All authority in heaven
and on earth has been given to me. Therefore go and make
disciples of all nations, baptizing them in the name of the
Father and of the Son and of the Holy Spirit, and teaching
them to obey everything I have commanded you.*

JUDGE NOT

I cannot judge another
  a sister or a brother;
I dare not say I'm right and you are wrong.
So many times I've failed Him
  for my sins were what nailed Him;
He shields me from the hell where I belong.
I cannot see what's inside
  things that in your heart reside;
God alone is the keeper of that key.
I have no right to condemn
  that right is reserved for Him;
And one day He will be the judge of me.
Each one will stand before Him
  we'll worship and adore Him;
The world will all bow down on bended knee.
He says to love each other
  each sister and each brother;
I won't judge you, and you should not judge me.

James 4:12

There is only one Lawgiver and Judge, the one who is able to save and destroy. But you---who are you to judge your neighbor?

John 13:34-35

A new command I give you: Love one another. As I have loved you, so you must love one another. By this all men will know that you are my disciples, if you love one another.

I'd Like To Believe

I'd like to believe that, if I had been there when Christ died,
I would not have been like Peter when three times he denied
That he knew Jesus.
I'd like to believe that, if Jesus had asked me to pray
As He sweated blood, preparing to go Calvary's way,
I would not have slept.
I'd like to believe that, if I had been ordered to hold
The hammer that nailed Him and caused such suffering untold,
I would have refused.
I'd like to believe that, had I been in Judas's shoes
And between Christ and a bag of silver I had to choose,
I would have chosen Christ.
I'd like to believe that, had I been told Christ was alive
And He had returned, though I knew He was crucified,
I would not have had doubts.
I'd like to believe that, if I had been that rich young man
And Christ asked me to give away my money and my land,
I would have given all.
I'd like to believe that I'm not the one who did all those things…
Doubted, denied, sold out, and crucified the King of Kings,
But I am.

ROMANS 3:23

for all have sinned and fall short of the glory of God,

ISAIAH 53:5

*But he was pierced for our transgressions, he was crushed
for our iniquities; the punishment that brought us peace
was upon him, and by his wounds we are healed.*

THE CRUCIFIXION

Matthew 26:39

Going a little farther, he fell with his
face to the ground and prayed, "My
Father, if it is possible, may this
cup be taken from me.
Yet not as I will, but as you will."

JOHN 3:16

He thought me worthy to save.
    For God so loved...He gave.
His blood was a crimson red.
    For God so loved...He bled.
His mercy is deep and wide.
    For God so loved...He died.
He defeated all His foes.
    For God so loved...He rose.
His journey on earth was done.
    For God so loved...He won.
My transgressions He forgives.
    For God so loved...He lives.

I now have hope...for God so loved.

JOHN 3:16

For God so loved the world that he gave his one and only Son, that whoever believes in him shall not perish but have eternal life.

HOW COULD YOU PLANT THAT SEED?

Lord, I know you formed the hill
Upon which your Son died,
And I know it was your will
That He be crucified.

Lord, you grew the thorny vine
They placed upon His head,
And you made the bitter wine
When, "I thirst," Jesus said.

Lord, you made the wood they used
To build that rugged cross.
You knew He would be abused
So we'd not suffer loss.

Lord, you watched from Heaven above
And tended to that tree.
Your sweet Spirit, like a dove,
Grew it for Calvary.

Lord, you gave your only Son
As you had planned for years.
On that tree our victory's won,
But it's watered with your tears.

**Lord, you made those foolish men
Who did that cruel deed.
How it must have hurt you when
You had to plant that seed.**

---

1 CORINTHIANS 1:18

For the message of the cross is foolishness to those who are perishing, but to us who are being saved it is the power of God.

HE WASHED THEIR FEET

John 13

Jesus Christ knew this would be the last night they would share
An earthly meal together, and He must now prepare
These men that He had chosen to carry out his plan
To spread the Gospel story and His great love for man.
So He removed his robe, wrapped a towel 'round his waist,
And knelt before each one of them with no hint of haste.
His hands were soft and tender; His countenance was sweet;
And like a lowly servant, He gently washed their feet.
Those twelve men He was cleansing just sat in disbelief,
But as their Savior touched them, they felt a sweet relief.
He knew they would face many challenges and woes
And that His earthly hours were drawing to a close.
He did not pass by Judas---the one He knew would be
The one who would betray Him as He faced Calvary.
When their eyes met, I wonder how Judas must have felt
As on the floor before him his master meekly knelt.
There He showed to the whole world the meaning of "forgive,"
And we must do the same if like Him we wish to live.
Peter did not understand, for how was he to know
How much he'd need that cleansing when he heard a rooster crow?
Christ showed them that their duty was to go out and serve
And tell the world of a grace that no one could deserve.
I'm thankful for that cleansing because it set me free.
Like Peter I am praying, "Oh, Lord, wash all of me!"

Out Into the Night

I often think of Judas and the choices that he made.
I also think of Jesus---knowing he would be betrayed.
Until that final moment, as Christ offered him some bread,
Judas could have changed his mind, staying with the Lord instead;
But as Judas ate the bread, Satan entered into him.
I know that, at that moment, Judas felt his world grow dim.
He turned his back on Jesus, choosing wrong instead of right,
Running from the light of grace, going out into the night.
How often are we guilty of just stumbling through the dark,
In search of worldly treasures as we fall short of the mark?
Life is so full of choices; we must keep our Lord in sight.
Hold to Him so you won't go straying out into the night.

JOHN 13:21-30

*After he had said this, Jesus was troubled in spirit and testified, "I
tell you the truth, one of you is going to betray me." His disciples
stared at one another, at a loss to know which of them he meant.
One of them, the disciple whom Jesus loved, was reclining next
to him. Simon Peter motioned to this disciple and said, "Ask him
which one he means." Leaning back against Jesus, he asked him,
"Lord, who is it?" Jesus answered, "It is the one to whom I will
give this piece of bread when I have dipped it in the dish." Then,
dipping the piece of bread, he gave it to Judas Iscariot, son of Simon.
As soon as Judas took the bread, Satan entered into him. "What
you are about to do, do quickly," Jesus told him, but no one at the
meal understood why Jesus said this to him. Since Judas had charge
of the money, some thought Jesus was telling him to buy what was
needed for the Feast, or to give something to the poor. As soon as
Judas had taken the bread, he went out. And it was night.*

THE JUDAS KISS

Lord, as the lips of Judas touched your face
And you knew so well what he came to do,
But you willingly went to take my place
And endure the pain mankind put you through,

How it must have hurt deep within your heart.
For betrayal cuts us so very deep,
Though you knew the plan---that you must depart
So you could rise again from death's cold sleep.

Still, betrayal brings such a bitter sting
When it comes from one we have called a friend.
The very ones who proclaimed you their King
Denied and betrayed you---that's hard to mend.

Lord, when I falter in the ways you taught
And I aim for the mark but often miss,
Remind me the price of my soul you bought;
Keep me from the guilt of a Judas kiss.

MATTHEW 26:48-49

*Now the betrayer had arranged a signal with them; "The
one I kiss is the man; arrest him." Going at once to Jesus,
Judas said, "Greetings, Rabbi!" and kissed him.*

THE NINTH HOUR

This moment He had dreaded kneeling in Gethsemane,
As He prayed to His Father, "Please let this cup pass from me!
But Father, if you will it, I am willing---lead me now.
I'm prepared for the beatings and the thorns upon my brow.
I can face the pain they cause to my side and nail-pierced hand;
But to face that ninth hour---Father, give me strength to stand...
To feel the sin of all men and be draped in guilt and blame
As I see you turn away from your Son covered in shame."

His cross had been so heavy as He stumbled up that hill.
The hours blurred with His pain; now the world grew dark and still.
He knew that in a moment, as the sky turned bleak and black,
He would face His hardest task; there would be no turning back.
As He faced that ninth hour and He could not hear or see
His father up in heaven that He needed desperately,
He called out to His Father, "Why have you forsaken me?"
Then He knew this ninth hour was the worst of Calvary.

Oh, Jesus, how I thank you for bearing all my sin
And struggling through a battle that you knew I could not win.
Because you gave everything and saw your journey through,
I won't have to feel the pain that ninth hour held for you.

MATTHEW 27:46

*About the ninth hour Jesus cried out in a loud voice,
"Eloi, Eloi, lama sabachthani?"---which means, "My
God, my God, why have you forsaken me?"*

Who Will Roll the Stone Away?

There was a stone that often blocked my way;
It was made of pride, selfishness and such.
It kept me in a tomb filled with decay...
Some rotting things nobody dared to touch.
I was wrapped in cloths of all-consuming sin;
The walls were made of fear as hard as rock.
A stone of self-destruction kept me in...
A seal so strong no mortal could unlock.
I wondered who could roll that stone away,
If I would ever be free of that place.
I found that all I had to do was pray,
And the stone was moved by something called grace.

MARK 16:2-4

*Very early on the first day of the week, just after sunrise,
they were on their way to the tomb and they asked each
other, "Who will roll the stone away from the entrance of
the tomb?" But **when they looked up**, they saw that the
stone, which was very large, had been rolled away.*

What Happened to His Cross?

I wonder what happened to the cross that was used for the crucifixion of Christ? Where are the three nails that secured His hands and feet to that cross? How and where did they dispose of used crosses? Were they ever reused? Somehow I cannot imagine that Christ's cross was ever used for anyone except Him. In my mind, that was holy wood to be used only by His Holiness.

His precious blood that stained that cross and those nails was priceless, and it could not have been casually tossed aside on a trash heap. I like to imagine that, after the body of Christ was removed, the cross, nails and blood were taken up into Heaven and stored in God's trophy case. There it stands in wondrous splendor, ruggedly beautiful. I think it will be standing there when we are standing before the throne of God. Wouldn't it be more than wonderful if God would allow each one of His children to kneel and touch the foot of that old rugged cross?!!!

1 Corinthians 1:18

For the message of the cross is foolishness to those who are perishing, but to us who are being saved it is the power of God.

1 Corinthians 15:57

But thanks be to God! He gives us the victory through our Lord Jesus Christ.

I WANT TO SEE HIS HANDS

When I get to Heaven amid choruses and bands,
I will ask my Jesus, "Please let me see your hands."
I want to see those hands that shed precious blood for me.
I want to see those hands that were scarred on Calvary.
I want to see those hands that have held me when I've cried.
I want to see those hands that forgave me when I lied.
I want to see those hands that lifted me each time I fell.
I want to see those hands that saved my soul from hell.
I want to see those hands that built the cornerstone.
I want to see those hands that claimed me for their own.
I want to see those hands that folded in prayer for me.
I want to see those hands that allowed me to go free.
I want to see those hands that found me when I strayed.
I want to see those hands that marked my debts all paid.
I want to see those hands that fed the multitude.
I want to see those hands that knew James and John and Jude.
I want to see those hands that turned water into wine.
I want to see those hands that caused the stars to shine.
I want to see those hands that taught dear Paul to see.
I want to see those hands that cured some of leprosy.
I want to see those hands that raised Lazarus from the dead.
I want to see those hands that Satan learned to dread.
I want to see those hands that calmed the angry sea.
I want to see those hands that reached way down for me.
I want to see those hands that always pled my case.
I want to see those hands, and I want to see His face.

◇◇◇

LUKE 23:46(B)

…"Father, into your hands I commit my spirit."…

◇◇◇

IF I WERE THE ONLY ONE

Yes, God would have sent his Son
Had I been the only one.
He'd have left his home above
If I were all He could love.
He would have hung on that tree
For sins committed by me.
He would have suffered and bled
For words I shouldn't have said.
That crown of thorns he'd have worn
If I alone had been born.
Those nails would have pierced his skin
If just my soul He would win.
He would have walked up that hill
If only my cup to fill.
The spear would have pierced his side
If only my soul to guide.
He'd have gladly born the shame
If just to keep me from blame.
He'd pray, "Not my will but Thine"
If all the world's sins were mine.
He'd save me from being defiled
If I were His only child.

---

1 PETER 2:24-25

*He himself bore our sins in his body on the tree, so that we might
die to sins and live for righteousness; by his wounds you have
been healed. For you were like sheep going astray, but now you
have returned to the shepherd and Overseer of your souls.*

In My Opinion

As I get older and remember how our country used to be, I start to think about how quickly we are changing---and not for the better. So many people are concerned with trying to be "politically correct" instead of trying to be "God correct." They want to be "people pleasers" instead of "God pleasers." The movies that are being produced and the themes of most television shows prove that the strong moral culture that once existed in America is now practically nonexistent. Our children are being exposed to things from which we were sheltered in the days of our youth, but today there is no way to completely shelter them short of locking them away in the attic. (I am fairly certain that is a criminal offense in itself.)

What is really disturbing is the fact that so many **churches** are trying so hard to be "politically correct" that they are overlooking actions that completely go against what God tells us in His Word. Yes, He does love sinners, and I am so very thankful He does. If He did not, there would be no one for Him to love, because we are all sinners; however, God hated sin so much that He sent His only Son to die an agonizing death to defeat it (John 3:16-17). We also are to love sinners, but we are not to love the sin. We are not to **condone** the sin. I looked up the word "condone" in a <u>Merriam-Webster Dictionary</u>, and the meaning is "to overlook or forgive, especially by treating (an offense) as harmless or trivial." Sin is neither harmless nor trivial in God's eyes, and neither should it be in ours. As the Apostle Paul felt about himself, I often feel as if I am the worst sinner that ever lived (1 Timothy 1:15-16). We are all sinners and fall short of the glory of God, according to Romans 3:23; but we have been given the full armor of God (Ephesians 6:10-18) with which to fight in the battle of spiritual warfare. During this time in history, we must all constantly wear our battle gear! The battle is perhaps coming to its climax during our days, and we must decide for which side we are willing to fight.

Family values are declining. Morality is disappearing. Church attendance is decreasing. Too many excuses for sin are being made. The church's silence has gone on too long. It is now or never!!! Rise up, oh Church of God, and stand for God and His Word!

WHILE THE CHURCH IS SLEEPING

Our children we are losing
Down pathways they are choosing.
Their loved ones are now weeping
While the Church is sleeping.

Our country is now falling
And will not hear God's calling.
For our sins we are reaping
While the Church is sleeping.

Morality's disappearing
While Satan's team is cheering.
The flames of hell are leaping
While the Church is sleeping.

Our leaders are forsaking
God's laws they should be making,
His Word man is not keeping
While the Church is sleeping.

God's people are not staying
Down on their knees and praying.
And souls in hell are heaping
While the Church is sleeping.

**When they were crucifying
Our Lord as He was dying,
And from Him blood was seeping,
Jesus was not sleeping.**

REVELATION 3:1-3

These are the words of him who holds the seven spirits of God and the seven stars. I know your deeds; you have a reputation of being alive, but you are dead. Wake up! Strengthen what remains and is about to die, for I have not found your deeds complete in the sight of my God. Remember, therefore, what you have received and heard; obey it, and repent. But if you do not wake up, I will come like a thief, and you will not know at what time I will come to you.

Why Were There Three Crosses?

In the beginning there were three Beings in one---the Father, the Son, and the Holy Spirit. From before time "three" has been a very special number, and what could be more special than the occasion of our salvation? There were three crosses because we needed a "Middle Man" to form a bridge between God and us. There were three crosses because one represents those who reject Christ, as did one of the thieves; one represents those who accept Christ, as did the other thief; and one is for the One who gave us that choice.

LUKE 23:39-43

One of the criminals who hung there hurled insults at him: "Aren't you the Christ? Save yourself and us!" But the other criminal rebuked him. "Don't you fear God," he said, "since you are under the same sentence? We are punished justly, for we are getting what our deeds deserve. But this man has done nothing wrong." Then he said, "Jesus, remember me when you come into your kingdom." Jesus answered him, "I tell you the truth, today you will be with me in paradise."

NATURE

1 Chronicles 16:23

Sing to the LORD, all the earth; proclaim
his salvation day after day.

Luke 12:27

"Consider how the lilies grow. They do not labor
or spin. Yet I tell you, not even Solomon in all
his splendor was dressed like one of these."

CREATION

Oh, how beautiful are the things you created;
Each season displays its special kind of splendor.
You planned it all as the angels watched and waited;
You formed this wonderful world with hands so tender.

There is no way that we mortals can understand
How you knew us before the moment of each birth;
But we are certain we were fashioned by your hand,
And for your glory we were placed upon this earth.

We do not need to know the how or when or why
Or question you at all about the things you do.
All we need to know is on you we can rely,
And in every circumstance you will see us through.

GENESIS 1:1

In the beginning God created the heaven and the earth.

GENESIS 1:27

*So God created man in his own image, in
the image of God created he him.*

GENESIS 1:31(A)

*And God saw every thing that he had made,
and, behold, it was very good.*

SEASONS

Father, the seasons are changing from summer to fall.
This morning a gentle rain is falling as I recall
The many changing seasons of my life and my heart.
Some were happy days; at times my world was torn apart.
But through each day I rest assured you are by my side;
You provide a haven in which my soul can abide.
Though I know I have wasted so many precious days
When I forgot to talk to you and to give you praise,
I pray not one more day shall pass that I do not seek
Your guidance and your face---every day of every week.
For with your loving presence, there's nothing I can't face.
You have provided everything in the form of grace.

ECCLESIASTES 3: 1

*To every thing there is a season, and a time
to every purpose under the heaven:*

THE LEAVES

The leaves are falling this morning and drifting from the trees.
They can't hold on; they're blown away with just the slightest breeze.
Though once so green and vibrant with the hope of a new birth,
They are now all dry and withered and tumbling to the earth.
This reminds me of some people who can't seem to hang on.
They struggle through each day until all their strength is gone.
They're so much like those dead, dry leaves that turn from green to brown,
Because they give up everything and just come tumbling down.
They do not know, or will not see, they can live forever
By trusting in our Savior who will forsake them never.
We must not stand and wait until all the trees are bare.
We must reach out to lost souls who are falling everywhere;
And just as leaves are given new life and hope each spring,
Those lost souls can live once more if we bring them to the King.

1 CORINTHIANS 13:1

*What if I could speak all languages of humans and of
angels? If I did not love others, I would be nothing more
than a noisy gong or a clanging cymbal. (CEV)*

THE FOG

The fog is rolling in
As if to cover this world's sin.
It's spreading far and wide
Just as the sin it tries to hide.
It forms a heavy haze
To conceal all of Satan's ways.
Deception can't last long,
Because we know the right from wrong.
Our Lord will lift the fog
Before we're swallowed by sin's bog.
Just ask Him to stay near,
And He will make your vision clear.

DEUTERONOMY 11:16

*Be careful, or you will be enticed to turn away and
worship other gods and bow down to them.*

LUKE 21:8

*He replied: "Watch out that you are not deceived.
For many will come in my name, claiming, 'I am he,'
and, 'The time is near.' Do not follow them."*

THE SUN AND THE SON

God made a light to shine on Earth with love in every ray.
Without this light all living things would surely pass away.
It gives us warmth and helps things grow and changes night to day.
It's called the SUN.

God made another light to shine on Souls so cold and stark.
Without this Light we would be lost and stumbling through the dark.
He shines His light upon our sin---erases every mark.
He's called the SON.

God made these lights---the Sun and Son---because He knew we'd need
One to help our bodies grow and one our souls to feed.
One can feel no pain at all, but one for us did bleed.
Our victory's WON.

***

GENESIS 1:15

*"and let them be lights in the expanse of the
sky to give light on the earth."*

MARCH

It's March again, Lord, my favorite time of year;
I'm glad that was the month you chose to send me here.
It was the time my life began upon this earth,
And it is still the time the world gets a new birth.
I see new leaves and buds and hear birds in chorus.
So often we don't see your wonders before us.
Only you could create so many shades of green
And a sky crystal blue and place us here between.
I can see two red birds here this very morning;
Only you could give them such brilliant adorning.
Anyone who needs proof of your true existence
Can just look around to witness your consistence.
From day to day, week to week, and from year to year,
The days, the nights, the seasons prove that you are near.
Some say it was by accident this world exists;
They seem to take such pride in being pessimists.
I pray they will realize before it's too late
So they won't be denied the entrance through your gate.
Why some do not believe, I just don't understand;
Each day I see proof of a mighty unseen hand.

ACTS 14:17

Yet he has not left himself without testimony. He has shown kindness
by giving you rain from heaven and crops in their seasons; he
provides you with plenty of food and fills your hearts with joy.

THE HARVEST

If every cotton boll
Represented one lost soul
And every grain of wheat
Was a soul facing defeat
And each kernel of corn
Was a soul to be reborn
And every single bean
A soul longing to be clean
And every grain of rice
Was a soul held in sin's vice
And every stalk of maize
A soul blinded by sin's haze
 And the grains of barley
Souls in Satan's hands so gnarly
And every pod of peas
Lost souls drifting in the breeze,
To achieve a high yield
We'd need workers in God's field.
God says this is the case
It's His harvest we must face
To gather them all in
Before souls are lost to sin.

MATTHEW 9: 37-38

*Then he said to his disciples, "The harvest is plentiful
but the workers are few. Ask the Lord of the harvest,
therefore, to send out workers into his harvest field."*

THIS IS THE DAY

I'm tired today
My body's sore
I tried to pray
A frown I wore

I've hills to climb
My spirit's weak
I have no time
His face to seek

I don't feel well
I'm grumpy, too
As you can tell
I've much to do

My temper's short
My tongue is sharp
I know I wart
I know I harp

My mood is bad
But now I see
What if He had
No time for me

For I should sing
A song of praise
Unto my king
All of my days

What comes my way
If sun or shade
This is the day
The Lord has made

PSALM 118:24

This is the day the Lord has made: let us rejoice and be glad in it.

Flowers in the Weeds

The field is overgrown with weeds;
No tiller has been there.
They came from voluntary seeds;
They're spreading everywhere.

But looking closer I can see
A flower now and then.
They strive so hard to just stand free
And bloom where weeds have been.

They may not be great in number,
But still they struggle on.
They cannot be caught in slumber,
For soon they'll see the dawn.

This world is so much like that field
O'er grown with weeds of sin,
But there are some who will not yield
And just let Satan win.

So in faith they seek God's pardon;
Each to His will concedes,
And they bloom in Father's garden
Like flowers in the weeds.

MATTHEW 13:24-30

Jesus told them another parable: "The kingdom of heaven is like a man who sowed good seed in his field. But while everyone was sleeping, his enemy came and sowed weeds among the wheat, and went away. When the wheat sprouted and formed heads, then the weeds also appeared. The owner's servants came to him and said, 'Sir, didn't you sow good seed in your field? Where then did the weeds come from?' 'An enemy did this,' he replied. The servants asked him 'Do you want us to go and pull them up?' 'No,' he answered, 'because while you are pulling the weeds, you may root up the wheat with them. Let both grow together until the harvest. At that time I will tell the harvesters: First collect the weeds and tie them in bundles to be burned; then gather the wheat and bring it into my barn.' "

FOR ALL OF GOD'S CHILDREN

Mark 10:15

I tell you the truth, anyone who will
not receive the kingdom of God like
a little child will never enter it.

JONAH

God told his prophet Jonah, "I have a task for you…
A most important mission that I want you to do.
Go to that city Nineveh and warn them of their fate.
They must repent and turn to me before it is too late."

Jonah said, "Those people are not worth my time today."
So he made up his mind to just turn and run away.
He thought he could make his plans of his own accord,
But Jonah soon discovered he could not outrun the Lord.

God sent a storm so violent it tossed his ship around.
Jonah was thrown overboard---so sure that he would drown.
God looked down in mercy and provided a large fish
That opened up its mouth and made Jonah his main dish.

Three days and nights old Jonah prayed, so sorry for his sin.
He thanked his Lord for saving him and vowed from deep within
That he would do his master's will without a frown or pout,
So the fish swam up to dry land and spit old Jonah out.

Jonah did as he was told and warned them of God's plan,
And every person turned to God, each woman, child, and man.
Jonah could not understand why God would show them grace,
For he forgot the grace God gave when he was in their place.

Don't let us be like Jonah and run from the tasks God gives.
Let us spread the message that our dear Savior lives.
Let all the world's salvation be our greatest wish
So God won't need to put us in the belly of that fish.

DAVID AND GOLIATH
(1 Samuel 17)

Goliath was a big man; he was a Philistine.
The sight of him in armor created quite a scene.
He was so full of himself, he boasted all around.
He said, "Send out your champion, if one is to be found!

If one you send can kill me, then we'll your servants be,
But if I win the battle, then you must bow to me."
The Israelites were frightened; King Saul was so dismayed.
They realized this conflict soon could not be delayed.

For forty days Goliath came forth and took his stand.
He dared them all to pass by his line drawn in the sand.
A shepherd boy named David had brought his brothers bread.
As he talked with his brothers, he heard what that man said.

David knew for Israel this was a great disgrace.
How could they let this big man get right up in their face?
When he was brought before Saul, young David told the king,
"Sir, please don't be discouraged. I'll fight this Philistine!"

Saul said, "You cannot do this, for you are much too young.
You'll be to him a small twig that he's picked up and flung."
Then David told of times when he'd fought a lion or bear
And rescued from their great jaws a lamb within his care.

David said, "The Lord who saved me from those beasts so mean
Is the same Lord I trust to defeat the Philistine."
Saul said to David, "Go, boy. May the Lord be with you."
Young David was determined; he knew what he must do.

Saul offered David armor and all his best for him,
But David soon discovered he could not fight in them.
He took them off and then he took his staff in his hand.
He placed five stones in his pouch, prepared to make his stand.

With his slingshot in his hand, he went to meet his foe.
Goliath cursed and threatened and warned him of much woe.
David said, "I do not fear your dagger, spear, or sword.
My victory is assured by the hand of our Lord."

David reached into his bag and pulled out one smooth stone.
He marched up to Goliath, a young boy scarcely grown.
He loaded up his slingshot; he aimed right for his head.
As the stone found its target, Goliath soon lay dead.

Sometimes we must face problems too large for us to bear,
But we can count on our Lord to share our every care.
No matter what the challenge, we can be bold and brave,
Because we trust that our Lord still has the power to save.

DANIEL AND THE LIONS' DEN

(Daniel 6)

Darius, a pagan king, took over Babylon.
Daniel was third over all; he worked hard and beyond.
King Darius had made plans to make Daniel the boss.
The two above him envied; it made them very cross.

They tried so hard to prove that this Daniel had some flaws,
But they could not find proof that would help them with their cause.
Their jealousy was so strong they came up with a plan.
They had the perfect scheme to help rid them of this man.

They went to King Darius and boasted of his worth.
They made him sound important---the greatest man on earth.
They convinced him that he should enforce a new decree
To insure that all would know of his great majesty.

For thirty days no one could request for anything
From any god or person, but only from the king.
If anyone disobeyed this new law made by men,
He would then be cast into the hungry lions' den.

King Darius signed the law with no way to repeal.
He never stopped to wonder how this made others feel.
Daniel heard about the law, but would not change his way.
He always prayed to his God three times in every day.

His enemies found Daniel as he prayed to his King.
They gladly rushed out to tell Darius everything.
Darius did all he could; Daniel was like his son.
The law said a king's decree just could not be undone.

Reluctantly Darius gave orders to his men.
Daniel was brought in and thrown into the lions' den.
He said to Daniel, "May your God save you if He will!"
The den was shut with a stone and marked with the king's seal.

King Darius could not sleep throughout that long dark night.
He ran toward the lions' den as soon as it was light.
He quickly called to Daniel, and then without a pause,
Daniel said, "The God I serve has shut the lions' jaws."

King Darius then sent to the world a new decree
That Daniel's God is mighty, and He can set us free.
No matter what the danger or beasts of life we face,
Daniel's God is our God, too, and we're saved by his grace.

NOAH AND THE ARK

Genesis 6-8

God made a man named Adam and his helpmate Eve,
Then Satan slithered in and taught them to deceive.
As years went by, man's wicked ways steadily increased.
God's heart was grieved, so He thought man's life should be ceased.

God had decided man should reap his just reward,
But Noah found favor in the eyes of his Lord.
Noah was a righteous man, blameless among men,
So God informed Noah that his world would soon end.

God told his servant Noah to gather cypress wood
And build an ark exactly as God said he should.
For God would send a flood to cover all the earth.
Noah and his family would start the world's rebirth.

So Noah did everything God told him to do.
All living creatures came; God sent them two-by-two.
Noah's friends laughed and said that he must be insane
To build an ark on land when they'd never seen it rain.

When the ark was ready, God gently shut them in;
The time was now at hand for raining to begin.
For forty days and nights the rain fell constantly,
'Til all but Noah's ark just vanished in the sea.

An olive branch was brought to Noah by a dove;
A new world was created by our God of love.
When God sends you a message, don't wait to reply.
Make sure your ark is ready, though the land is dry.

The Rich Man and Lazarus
Luke 16:19-31

Lazarus lay just outside a very rich man's gate.
He begged for just a few crumbs from the rich man's plate.
Lazarus was so sick that dogs came and licked each sore.
The rich man in his purple robe chose to just ignore.

This poor downtrodden beggar was not worth his time of day.
It was so easy for him to just look the other way.
Then one happy day Lazarus went to meet his Lord,
And all of Heaven's riches on Lazarus were poured.

Soon the rich man died, and he met an awful fate.
At last he recognized his sin, but it was now too late.
He looked toward Heaven and he saw the man whom he had spurned,
And suddenly he realized the tables had been turned.

He prayed, "Oh Father Abraham, send Lazarus to me
With just one drop of water to help ease my agony."
Abraham replied to him, "Though your pain is severe,
The chasm is too deep and wide; we can't get there from here!"

The rich man said, "Dear Abraham, let me now implore;
Send Lazarus to my brothers to warn them what's in store.
If someone from the dead goes there, I know they will repent;
Then they'll escape the torment in this place where I was sent.

Abraham replied, "They already know God's Word;
Yet they live on in sinful ways as if they've never heard.
Even if dear Lazarus spoke up from his grave,
They would not heed the warning but refuse the grace God gave."

Even in our world today the story is the same.
So many souls are lost and still live in sin and shame.
God has so many blessings waiting for us to receive.
Our Savior died and rose again, yet some still won't believe.

SAMSON AND DELILAH
Judges 13:1-16:31

A woman had gone childless for all her married life;
She could not be a mother---only her husband's wife.
Then she received a visit from God's own messenger.
The angel had been sent out with such good news for her.

He told her that she would soon give birth to her own son,
And this boy had been chosen to be a special one.
He would be a Nazirite from birth 'til he was dead,
And no one was to ever cut one hair on his head.

She named her baby Samson; God's spirit was in him.
He stayed close to his parents, then one day he told them,
"A young Philistine woman is whom I want to wed."
They told their son that he should choose someone else instead.

Marriage to a Philistine would be against God's law.
They asked their son if he would this one request withdraw,
But Samson still insisted, "She's the right one for me."
His parents then consented, though they did not agree.

Then on his way to Timnah to see his future wife,
A lion charged at Samson, but Samson took his life.
Sometime at a later date, he traveled that same path.
He came across the carcass left over from his wrath.

A swarm of bees and honey lay in the lion that day,
And he scooped out some honey to eat along the way.
Then Samson made a riddle about what he had found
And wagered with some guests at his wedding feast in town.

The thirty men were angry and threatened Samson's wife.
They threatened all her family and said they'd take her life
If she did not coax Samson and cry 'til she could get
The answer to his riddle so they could win the bet.

Samson's wife kept pestering the poor man night and day
Until he let his guard down and let her have her way.
He told his wife the answer; then she told all those men.
So Samson had to pay up to those she'd helped to win.

Samson left his brand new wife to let his anger mend.
While he was gone, her father gave her to Samson's friend.
Samson went to claim his bride and learned what had occurred.
He vowed to hurt the Philistines, and Samson kept his word.

He caught three hundred foxes and tied them two-by-two,
Then tied a torch onto them. He knew what he must do.
So Samson lit the torches and burned the fields of grain
And olive groves and vineyards. He caused those people pain.

The Philistines were angry and burned his wife to death.
Samson swore to get revenge; he vowed with every breath.
Three thousand men from Judah went up to Samson's cave
To beg him to surrender and thus their town to save.

Samson allowed those people to bind him with two ropes
And lead him to the Philistines where he would dash their hopes.
He found a donkey's jawbone and slew a thousand men,
For God gave him the power it took for him to win.

Samson guided Israel for twenty years or so,
Then Samson met Delilah who brought him pain and woe.
Four times she begged of Samson, "Please tell me of the source
Of all your strength and power." She nagged 'til she was hoarse.

The first three times he fooled her and filled her head with lies.
The fourth time he told the truth; that wasn't very wise.
He told her if she shaved off his hair onto the floor,
He'd be like any mortal and would be strong no more.

Delilah had made a pact with Philistines for pay.
She had a man shave off his braids as on her lap he lay.
Then she called out to Samson, "The Philistines are here!"
He did not know he had lost his seven braids so dear.

The Philistines then seized him, and they gouged out his eyes.
Oh, Samson, foolish Samson, why couldn't you be wise?
As his vision left him, and his world was growing dim,
Samson did not realize that his Lord had left him.

They took him down to Gaza and put on quite a show,
But somehow no one noticed his hair began to grow.
As they were celebrating, they had Samson brought in,
For he was entertainment in their vile world of sin.

Samson said to the servant who led him by the hand,
"Put me between two pillars where I can lean and stand."
The temple was so crowded with Philistines galore;
Thousands were upon the roof and thousands on the floor.

Samson prayed unto the Lord, "Please give me strength once more.
Give me revenge for my eyes and the evil acts before."
He reached out and braced his hands where central pillars stood.
He asked God to let him die, and God said that he could.

Samson pushed with all his might with power from above,
And he brought down that temple with one last mighty shove.
Though Samson was not always the wisest of all men,
God can take our weaknesses and make us strong again.

THE LOAVES AND THE FISHES
John 6:1-15

Jesus reached the far shore of the Sea of Galilee.
A crowd of people followed because they wished to see
More of his great miracles and healing of the sick.
He went up the mountainside above that crowd so thick.

When Jesus looked up and saw the crowd approaching him,
He turned to ask of Philip, "What bread shall we feed them?"
This was, of course, just a test to hear what Philip said,
For Jesus knew the answer as to the source of bread.

Philip replied to Jesus, "If we used eight months' pay,
It would not buy one small bite for everyone today."
Then Andrew, Peter's brother, told them of one young boy
Who had a small lunch with him that he planned to enjoy.

He had five small barley loaves and also two small fish,
But how could that scant portion make up so large a dish?
There must have been five thousand who needed to be fed.
How could they satisfy them with such few fish and bread?

Jesus said, "Have them sit down." He took the loaves they'd found.
He gave thanks to His Father; then he passed it around.
He took the fish and blessed it, and shared it as before,
And each one ate until full, yet there was plenty more.

Christ said to his disciples, "Now gather up the part
That still remains uneaten---more now than at the start."
They gathered up twelve baskets filled to the top with bread.
"Surely this is our Prophet!" five thousand people said.

Christ knew this was not the time for Him to be named king.
He withdrew to be alone and ponder everything.
That same king who managed to five thousand people feed
Is the One who still today can meet our every need.

THE PRODIGAL SON
Luke 15:11-32

Once a father had two sons and loved them both the same.
The younger son came to him and boldly did proclaim
That he desired his portion of what was his due share.
His father gave it to him; he wanted to be fair.

Soon that younger son left home and wasted all he had.
He did not have one thing left that he got from his dad.
A famine came to the land, and he was soon in need.
He took a job tending pigs and pouring out their feed.

He soon became so hungry the pig's food did look good.
He longed to see his father, and wondered if he should.
He summoned all his courage and headed back toward home,
For he had learned his lesson as he began to roam.

All through that entire journey, he practiced what he'd say.
He rehearsed his mournful speech each step along the way.
"Father, I have sinned against heaven and earth and you.
Please let me be your servant." Then home came into view.

He was still a long way off when father spied his son.
His father's heart was joyful, and he began to run.
He grabbed his son and kissed him as tears shone in his eyes.
He scarcely heard his son say, "Dad, I apologize."

The father called his servants and gave them this command,
"Bring the best robe and sandals. Put a ring on his hand.
You must kill the fattened calf; together we will dine.
Though he was lost, now he's found, this younger son of mine!"

The older son was working out in the fields near home.
He heard music and dancing and asked, "What's going on?"
They told him that his brother was back from his sojourn,
And father celebrated for his son's safe return.

The older son was angry and thought of time he'd spent
Doing what he thought was right. So now he did resent
The way his father acted over his younger son.
He seemed to have forgotten the evil things he'd done.

The son refused to enter the place the meal was served.
He did not wish to join in a feast so undeserved.
His father came out to him and begged him to come in.
The son said, "In you service is where I've always been.

I've never disobeyed you; I did not boast nor gloat.
Yet you never shared with me---not even one small goat.
Now this son who turned away and left your heart to grieve
Returns to find that you will with open arms receive."

"My son," the father told him, "you're always here with me.
Everything I have is yours, just ask and it will be;
But I had lost your brother to sin and grief and strife.
Now he's found his way back home and gone from death to life."

We have that kind of father who lets us choose our way
Then patiently stands listening to hear His children say,
"My Father, I have hurt you and spent my time with sin."
He opens wide his arms and says, "Child, just come on in."

THE GOOD SAMARITAN
Luke 10:30-37

While walking from Jerusalem on down to Jericho,
A man was stopped by robbers who sought to bring him low.
They took his clothes and beat him and left him there for dead.
It seemed he held onto life by just a slender thread.

A priest walked down that same road, and when he saw the man,
He walked to the other side without a helping hand.
Then a Levite passed that way and saw the man in need.
He likewise just passed on by and paid the man no heed.

Now Samaritans and Jews were not the best of friends;
They did not like each other and seldom made amends.
But then a Samaritan came riding down that road.
When he saw the Jewish man, he set aside his load.

This man had a tender heart with pity for another.
He vowed to himself that day, "I'll treat him like a brother."
He took out his oil and wine that he had with him there
And poured it on every wound and bandaged them with care.

His donkey stood there waiting to carry his next load.
The injured man was placed there then led on down the road.
That despised Samaritan took that man to an inn.
He gently took good care of him as if he were his kin.

The next day, before he left, two silver coins he paid
To make sure the innkeeper would give the poor man aid.
He said, "Please look after him. I'll come back to your door,
Then I will reimburse you if I should owe you more."

From this we learn a lesson about how we should live.
God sees deep within our hearts and knows the love we give.
Our neighbors are all mankind that God sends from above,
And He expects all of us to show our neighbors love.

SHADRACH, MESHACH
AND ABEDNEGO
Daniel 3

King Nebuchadnezzar said, "Oh, people, hear me now!
Before this golden idol, you every one must bow!
If you refuse to worship, the punishment is dire!
Your body will be picked up and thrown into that fire!"

Now people from all nations were gathered all around,
And when the music sounded, they knelt upon the ground.
Astrologers came forward to tattle to the king.
"Three Jewish boys," they said, "are ignoring everything."

The king began a tirade in tones both loud and clear,
"Go bring Shadrach and Meshach and Abednego right here!"
When they arrived before him, the king gave his command.
He warned them of the furnace so they would understand.

The boys replied to the king, "This act we cannot do.
We serve a God most powerful; and, Sir, it is not you.
Our Lord can rescue us today. He has the power to save;
But even if He does not, we have the strength He gave.

No matter what the outcome, we will not bow to you;
So go ahead and finish whatever you must do."
The king then gave his order to fuel up the fire,
Made it seven times hotter; flames were leaping higher.

The soldiers bound God's servants and tossed them to the fire.
It was so hot the soldiers did every one expire.
As Nebuchadnezzar looked into the fiery blaze,
He could not believe his eyes, for he was too amazed.

He said, "I know there were three that we tossed through that door;
But in that fire, safe and free, I know that I see four!"
As he approached the furnace, he gave a mighty shout!
He ordered, "Shadrach, Meshach, and Abednego, come out!"

As the three young men stepped out, no harm had come to them.
When the king saw what God did, he put his trust in Him.
As you recall this message, remember what they learned.
Just put your faith in our Lord, and you will not get burned.

*The road got progressively narrower as Balaam and his donkey continued on their journey. With each obstacle that appeared in the road, there was less and less room to maneuver around them. Finally, at the third and last obstacle, the donkey could do nothing but fall to her knees. I think that God has brought our country to that third obstacle in the road. America is facing many crises, and there is nowhere left to turn except to fall on our knees before our Lord. We must remember the lesson taught by Balaam's donkey and live by the message in **2 Chronicles 7:14**---If my people, who are called by my name, will humble themselves and pray and seek my face and turn from their wicked ways, then will I hear from heaven and will forgive their sin and will heal their land.*

BALAAM'S DONKEY

(Numbers 22:21-35)

Balaam and two servants rode toward Moab one fine day,
But God in his anger placed an angel in their way.
The donkey saw the angel and veered into a field.
Balaam beat his donkey until she was forced to yield.

Again God placed the angel to block old Balaam's path,
But Balaam could not see his Lord's messenger of wrath.
The donkey pressed against the wall that stood on either side,
And Balaam's foot was crushed, but so was Balaam's pride.

Once more he beat his donkey, with patience growing thin,
For still he could not see this reminder of his sin.
Again God's angel stood there within a space so tight
There was no room to turn to the left or to the right.

The donkey stopped and lay down with Balaam on her back.
He took his staff and beat her with such a mean attack.
Then God gave to the donkey the power of man's word,
And as she spoke to Balaam, this is what he heard.

"What have I done to you that you beat me three times so?"
Balaam said, "You mocked me when you refused to go.
If I had a sword, I would kill you where you stand."
"All these years," the donkey said, "I have followed your command."

The Lord opened Balaam's eyes; his heart began to race.
He saw the angel standing there and fell down on his face.
The angel then asked Balaam, "Why did you beat this beast?
She saw me and turned away and saved your life at least.

You'd have been slain by my sword had she not stepped aside.
Though I'd have spared the donkey, you surely would have died.
I came here to oppose you; your mindset is all wrong.
You must repeat just what I say to that Moab throng."

Balaam said, "Yes, I have sinned. I could not see you there.
If you desire, I will go back. You gave me quite a scare."
The angel said to Balaam, "Go with these men today,
But when you speak at Moab, I'll tell you what to say."

> God sometimes uses creatures
> To "kick up" quite a fuss...
> Such unexpected teachers
> To make a point to us.

2 Chronicles 7:14

If my people, who are called by my name, will

(3 requirements of us)
1. humble themselves and pray

2. and seek my face

3. and turn from their wicked ways

(3 promises from God)
1. then will I hear from heaven

2. and will forgive their sin

3. and will heal their land

WE

PRAY---------------------------------------HEAR

SEEK---------------------------------------FORGIVE

TURN---------------------------------------HEAL

GOD

This is the only way to bring our country out of the mess it is in. This country was founded on God. We are allowing a few of Satan's followers to take God out of our land. When God is removed from America, our foundation is gone, and so is our country, as we know it.

CHRISTMAS

Luke 2:10-11

But the angel said to them, "Do not be afraid. I bring you good news of great joy that will be for all people. Today in the town of David a Savior has been born to you; he is Christ the Lord."

JOSEPH

Matthew 1:18-25

An angel came to me and spoke,
"Listen to me! This is no joke.
The great God above who sees us
Will send a boy you'll name Jesus."
I wondered why God would choose me;
This child would change eternity.
Now I did not know what to do
For my wife Mary was soon due.
I must find us a place to stay
Before his birth got underway.
In a stable the baby lay;
A king upon a bed of hay.
He smiled at me; it was a sign.
I'd raise this boy; he would be mine.
I'd teach him and I'd give him love
'Til he returned to God above.

MARY'S BOY

The road had been long and the light was dim
As the couple arrived in Bethlehem.
Joseph was worried about his young bride;
Where could they find a safe place to abide?
The city was crowded; there was no place
For the birth of our Lord, the King of Grace.
But Mary knew while there in Bethlehem
That her Lord would provide a place for them.
She knew that her God was more than able,
And He led them to a warm, dry stable.
While shielded there protected from danger,
She gently placed her son in a manger.
Shepherds came near as they followed a star;
They worshipped him after traveling far.
Then three wise men came with gifts for him,
For this infant king born in Bethlehem.
Even the animals gathered around;
They watched as he slept and made not a sound.
Joseph and Mary knew they had been blessed,
But I wonder if they could ever have guessed
The significance of this quiet birth
And what it would mean to people on earth?
They knew this was no ordinary child.
Did they know he would save a world defiled?
He came in the form of this tiny one
This King of Kings, God's begotten Son.
Through this small child, God had planned from the start
To offer salvation for every heart.
His path was laid out; He would do God's will.
God's every promise this babe would fulfill.
But on that night Mary thought not of this;
She cuddled her child and gave him a kiss.
Mary could not help but to be amazed

As on his sweet face she just smiled and gazed.
For this precious boy from God up above
Was filled with the light of his Father's love.
As Joseph rested, Mary held her boy;
She was filled with peace, contentment and joy.
She cherished each moment she shared with him.
Her sweet baby boy born in Bethlehem.

MY FRIEND

If I had known Jesus when he was a boy,
Would we have been friends? Would we have shared a toy?

Would we have played tag and many other games?
Would we have stood together when we got called names?

When bullies made threats, would we have stood up tall,
Knowing that together we could beat them all?

We would not need fists as in a normal fight;
Jesus knew all the words to tell them what's right.

Would we run in the sunshine---play in the dirt,
And lend some comfort if one of us got hurt?

What fun it would be to know Jesus back then
As just a young boy and my very best friend.

THE REASON FOR THE SEASON

Luke 2: 1-14

The scoffers and the doubters seem to grow from year to year.
They tell us that our Savior was never really here.
Though they celebrate the holiday and love the season,
They try to tell the world that Christ is not the reason.
They call it "*X-mas*" just as if it's some unknown item,
And they try to force the Christians to stand up and "fight 'em."
But we who know that baby boy who lay upon the hay
Are sure He *is* the reason that we have a *Christ*mas day.
Until they open up their hearts and let His love shine in,
There is no way they ever will completely comprehend
The love it took that special day two thousand years ago
When God sent down His special gift to this old world below.
The unbelievers think they have the whole thing figured out,
And so they try to fill the world with their own fears and doubt.
One day they'll stand before the throne as God opens His Book.
He'll turn the pages one by one, and then He'll take a look.
The scoffers and the doubters will all bow on bended knee
When God shows them the *X's* written where their names should be.

There Is No Room

When our Savior was born in Bethlehem,
This sinful old world had no room for Him.
The innkeeper tried to send them away;
They had no room for the Christ Child that day.

He traveled throughout this wilderness land
To save a world that did not understand.
For thirty-three years He lived as a man,
Then ended life here just as it began.

Today as we hustle and race about,
So often it seems we still shut Him out.
We open the door to despair and gloom
Each time that we tell Him, "There is no room."

LUKE 2:6-7

*While they were there, the time came for the baby to
be born, and she gave birth to her firstborn, a son. She
wrapped him in cloths and placed him in a manger,
because there was no room for them in the inn.*

JUST SOME THOUGHTS

Psalm 111:2

Great are the works of the LORD; they are
pondered by all who delight in them.

Thoughts from the Laundromat

I was at the laundromat in Judsonia, Arkansas, once again. When I was changing paper money into quarters at a change machine outside, I noticed that it short-changed me one quarter. For some reason it always bothers me to be short-changed---even if it is only twenty-five cents; however, this time I decided to take a different look at being "cheated." I thought about how God always works EVERYTHING for the good of those who love and trust Him (Romans 8:28), so I decided to see if perhaps that quarter would be returned sometime, somewhere that day. It was just a fanciful thought, and I smiled as the notion drifted quietly through my mind.

About thirty or forty minutes later, as I was removing some wet jeans from a washing machine to place them into a dryer, I saw a penny lying on the bottom of the washing machine. I thought, "Well, there is part of the quarter I lost." Then, as I moved another pair of jeans, there lay a quarter underneath them. "Wow!" I thought to myself, "God did not just return the quarter---He returned twenty-six cents." Even though the money in the washing machine came from jeans that belonged to us, I still considered it to be "found money." I was pleased. God is GOOD!

A short while later, as I sat reading while the dryers were running, the owner (or manager?) of the building came in and unexpectedly gave me a gold-colored token for the car wash area next door. I asked him if the car wash used tokens instead of quarters, and he said that it accepted either but that the token was worth four quarters. It was a gift from him to me in appreciation for being a laundromat customer. Now I had an unexpected $1.26 in place of the quarter that was lost. God is VERY GOOD!

After loading my fresh, clean laundry into my vehicle, I walked around to the driver's side to get in. Something on the pavement at my feet caught my eye. It was a 1982 penny---heads up. The total was now $1.27. It is so true that God always gives us more than we could ever lose. What an AWESOME GOD we serve!

FOUR A.M.

There is something surreal about sitting outside at four o'clock in the morning waiting for a family pet to answer his "call of nature." It is at such times that a person can really sense the presence of God Himself. There we sit, God and I, watching a puppy move around the yard looking for just the "right spot." Somehow the ambiance is just not the same during daylight hours as it is at four in the morning. I have learned through various experiences that I am never alone. God is with me wherever I may be, but it is just such times as this that I am most aware of Him. Maybe God's presence is so noticeable at that time because I can finally "be still and know" that HE IS GOD.

PSALM 16:11

You have made known to me the path of life; you will fill me with joy in your presence, with eternal pleasures at your right hand.

Reflections from the Laundromat

Near Jerusalem
Luke 19:11

While they were listening to this, he went on to tell them a parable, because he was near Jerusalem and the people thought that the kingdom of God was going to appear at once.

From the moment of our births, we all begin our journey toward Jerusalem. Christ knew that his earthly life was coming to an end in Jerusalem, and He made the most of the thirty-three years He spent here. Some of our journeys are brief...some are longer. Some people feel their journeys are too brief, while others feel their journeys are too long...they begin to yearn for "home." However long our stay on earth may be, each step we take and each breath we breathe brings us closer to our own Jerusalem. I pray that we will all be ready for our next journey when we get there.

Trailer Trash?

Yesterday I watched a movie on TV in which they mentioned the term "trailer trash." I have never been fond of that term. For one thing, some of the best people I've met have lived in mobile homes (commonly known as "trailers"). Actually, I'm not sure how they came to be known as trailers. Maybe it's because they can be pulled behind a vehicle. Part of the dictionary definition of "trailer" is "a vehicle equipped to serve wherever parked as a dwelling or place of business." It is also "a vehicle that is hauled by another vehicle." Personally, I prefer the name "mobile home." After all, if home really is "where the heart is," then it most assuredly should be mobile. Just as a church is not a building, neither is a home a building. Both the church and the home consist of people, not bricks and mortar. When we married, we lived in a mobile home "trailer" for nearly six years. (It was twelve feet by forty-four feet in size.) We brought both of our children "home" to that trailer. Now, over forty years later, we spend most of our time in an RV camper at various RV parks. My husband's work requires this. I guess some people might say that we stay "away from home" the majority of the time. We say that we are home.

PHILIPPIANS 4:12-13

I know what it is to be in need, and I know what it is to have plenty. I have learned the secret of being content in any and every situation, whether well fed or hungry, whether living in plenty or in want. I can do everything through him who gives me strength.

GRAFFITI

As I sat waiting for a freight train to pass along the track in front of my automobile, the thought came to me that my life has been very similar to the cars crawling by covered with various kinds of graffiti. Some of the multi-colored scenes decorating the cars of the train were beautiful, while others were ugly and almost scary. Just as some human hands made the beautiful scenes, so have some humans helped to make the beautiful days of my life. Likewise, humans often help create the ugly, scary days for some people. I am thankful that I have not had many of those days.

I often think, "It's just not fair!" Often it seems that the ugly graffiti far outweighs the beautiful. Why is it that we notice the "ugly" much more than the "beautiful"? Why is so much emphasis placed on the ugly? Why is so much energy exerted worrying about the ugly? Why are so many tears spilled because of the ugly? Why do we waste so much of life because of the ugly? Where is the faith we need to overcome the ugly?

I suppose that it is the graffiti of our lives that gives us balance. As it has always been said, without the ugly we could not fully appreciate the beautiful. Scene after scene is woven together until our "train of life" is finished and we pull into the final station at the throne of our God. He is the only one who really knows how and why the pieces fit together as they do. There is a pattern to it all---His pattern---and that is all we need to know. He is the artist and we are the canvas. He paints the beautiful scenes; but we so often allow the world to encroach on our canvas, and that is when the ugly scenes appear. He holds the brushes of Heaven, while Satan holds the brushes of hell. It is our choice as to which brush we choose to decorate our lives.

Why don't we notice the beautiful more and the ugly less? Why can't we realize that the beautiful moments far outnumber the ugly ones? Why do we take the beautiful for granted? Why can't we SEE the beautiful?

Treasure In The Trunk

There are some things that I will always wonder about. Some of them never happened because they were out of my control, while other events never came to fruition because of my fear.

Once at a "Trader's Village" flea market in Texas I saw a trunk sitting in the center of one of the walkways. A note taped to the top of the trunk declared that whatever was inside was "Free." No one stopped to check it out, including me. I walked past that trunk several times wanting to open it to see what was inside, but I never did because I was afraid.

Afraid of what??? Maybe that it was empty and I would be laughed at because I should have known that this world offers us nothing for free. (God is the only One who gives us so many gifts for free.) Maybe that it contained something absolutely absurd that I would be obligated to keep and I would be embarrassed. Maybe that the trunk contained something alive that would frighten me.

For whatever reason---or perhaps for all of the above-mentioned reasons---I never found the courage to open that trunk. Now, many years later, I still wonder from time to time just what that trunk contained. I think that maybe it was some piece of merchandise from a nearby booth since the people there seemed to be responsible for it. Perhaps there was a one hundred dollar bill inside. Maybe it was empty. Because of my fear of embarrassment or humiliation or merely fear of fear itself, I will never know the identity of the treasure inside the trunk. How many other treasures have I missed because of fear?

JOSHUA 1:9

Have I not commanded you? Be strong and courageous.
Do not be terrified; do not be discouraged, for the LORD
your God will be with you wherever you go.

Broken In The Garden

Paradise was broken in the garden.
Adam blamed Eve and God, who gave him the woman.
Eve blamed the serpent.
The serpent slithered away on his belly in the dust.
The apple was innocent…if it were actually an apple. The Scripture does not
state that it was.

Love was broken last week by words as sharp as the serpent's fangs.
Words from a wayward child finally caused something to snap and break into
two estranged pieces.
That feeling that once existed is now gone.
I suppose self-preservation finally kicked in.
A feeling of numbness is far better than pain…the constant pain that was
felt for so long.
It is a feeling of release from a very heavy burden.

Paradise was restored in another garden called Gethsemane.
The serpent's head was finally and eternally crushed.
Yet, the pathway back to Paradise is strewn with hurts and hang-ups that were
originally unnecessary.
It is a different form of paradise.

That particular love that was broken will never return.
Perhaps something similar to it will take its place, but it will not be the same.
When there is a feeling once more, it will be **a different form of love**.

Helpless to Help

It is hard to accept the fact that some people you love just cannot be helped, no matter how much you desire to do so. God could intervene, but He will not, because of something He gave to us humans called "free will." The mind certainly is a battlefield where forces of good and evil are constantly at war, and unless a person is ready and willing to choose "good," there is really nothing any other human can do about it.

So many times we are forced to stand helplessly by and watch someone we love destroy themselves with drugs, alcohol, pornography, obesity, depression, and on and on and on. We pray constantly that he will survive long enough to come to his senses. Sometimes he does and sometimes he doesn't. However it goes, we cannot blame God or ourselves when we have done all we can do and given all we can give to help someone who refuses to help himself.

We all have addictions of one kind or another. We are all born seeking for something that we instinctively know is missing from our lives. When we seek for this missing piece in the wrong places, our destructive addictions develop. Until we learn to seek God every day and to seek His will for our lives, we will continue to be addicted to the harmful things that plague us in this world. We cannot find answers anywhere except in the presence of the One who has all of the answers. "Seek and ye shall find." It really does not matter if we get the answers now or later. They will come, according to His timetable.

MATTHEW 7:7

"Ask and it will be given to you; seek and you will find; knock and the door will be opened to you."

JUST A STUMP

One afternoon when Daddy came in from school, he had a black eye and a few scrapes and bruises. He had been in a fight with another boy that day, but he did not want his daddy to know about it. When Grandpa asked him what had happened, he replied, "I ran into a stump." Grandpa didn't question him anymore about the incident, but I am fairly certain that he knew the truth before he asked.

A short time later, Daddy came in after school another day looking pretty much as he had looked the first time. Without hesitating, Grandpa looked at him and asked, "What happened, Bob? Did you run into that same stump?"

How many times do we think we can outsmart our parents who have already failed at trying to outsmart their parents who have already failed to outsmart their parents and on and on down the family line? Why do we even try? Likewise, why do we think we can fool God with our pitiful stories or excuses when He is the One who knows us best? How God must laugh at us as we rack our brains trying to come up with some halfway believable tale that we think will fool Him.

Remember, our parents are wise, but God is much wiser. He is all knowing, all understanding, and all forgiving. How long can we go on thinking that we can pull the wool over God's eyes? How can we actually believe that we can keep secrets from Him? How can we think for one moment that He can't see the wrongs we do? Remind me, dear Lord, that I cannot hide anything from you---and never should I want to do so.

PSALM 139:1-3

O Lord, you have searched me and you know me. You know when I sit and when I rise; you perceive my thoughts from afar. You discern my going out and my lying down; you are familiar with all my ways.

NO SHOES

My daddy was born in 1923, so he attended elementary school many years ago. One of my favorite memories about which he often told us happened on his way home from school one afternoon during a cold part of the year. Back in his day, the boys wore short pants with long stockings and sturdy shoes. As he recalled it, he often removed his shoes and stockings shortly after arriving at school.

Unable or reluctant to replace his long stockings or shoes at the end of the school day, Daddy often walked home barefoot. On that particular afternoon, a man who knew Daddy's family stopped and asked why he was walking home in that cold weather without any shoes on his feet. Daddy replied, "Papa won't buy me no shoes."

Needless to say, when this meeting was related to his papa, Daddy got a whipping he was not soon to forget. Knowing my daddy, however, I am very sure that it did not change his habit for very long.

How often do we live lives that seem to indicate to others that we have a Father who does not provide for our needs? When other people observe us on a day-to-day basis, what impression do we give them about the faithfulness and generosity of our Heavenly Father? When we face hardships and heartaches, do we face them in such a manner that those observing us know without a doubt that we do have a Father upon whom we can rely to fulfill all our needs?

We should strive to be like the apostle Paul and be content in all circumstances, knowing that we have a Father who provides for all of our needs. As the old saying goes, "God is never surprised." God never worries. Why should we?

PHILIPPIANS *4:11-12*

*I am not saying this because I am in need, for I have learned to
be content whatever the circumstances. I know what it is to be
in need, and I know what it is to have plenty. I have learned
the secret of being content in any and every situation, whether
well fed or hungry, whether living in plenty or in want.*

A Tragic Afternoon

When I was a very young girl, I remember one afternoon when tragedy struck down a dirt road that ran right behind our house. A black family lived in a small, wood-framed house on the left side just a short distance down that little dead-end road. Suddenly there was a great commotion, and people were running toward that little house. It had caught on fire and was quickly engulfed in flames. I remember some black people screaming and moaning, but I was not sure just what was going on. I was very young and seemed to be watching a play that I could not fully comprehend.

As people were trying to help all they could, it was disclosed that a baby was in the house. They could not get the baby out. I don't remember if the child was a boy or a girl, but I remember the devastating grief of the parents. I really don't know if the child had been left alone for a minute or if someone panicked and forgot to get him (or her) as they hurried to escape the inferno. No matter the reason, a tiny, brief life was gone that day never actually having had a chance to have a life.

So many children are lost in similar ways. We cannot understand the rhyme or reason of it all, and I suppose we were not intended to have that kind of understanding. That understanding is left to God alone, and we are not to question---although we often do. I really don't think He minds very much that we ask, "Why." I have always believed that there is a reason for everything, but we may never know that reason in this earthly life. Hard times help to build character, or so we are told. I suppose that is true, but I see hard times as steppingstones to a stronger faith. Sometimes God puts us in a position in which we have no other alternative than to lean solely on Him or to turn our backs on Him completely. It is our choice. How foolish it is not to choose Him! He knows the plan for our lives. He has the roadmap. He has the strength. He has the answers.

I have some dear friends who have lost children, and my heart continues to break for their heartache. I have seen tremendous demonstrations of their faith through such tragedies, and I can only hope that I could be that strong. As of this time, I have never lost a child. I pray that God takes me home before that ever happens, but I realize that that is nearly every parent's prayer. We must realize that our children are not actually "our children" but are only loaned to us for a few short years. That is easy to say, but we still want our children with us. Letting go is hard for most parents; but God gave them to us, and He will complete the plan He has for them.

Still, I sometimes recall that tragic afternoon down that little dirt road. It was close enough to our home to reach that house in a matter of moments. Most of my memories of home are pleasant; however, like most of life, the bad must blend in with the good. I am just so very thankful that "God is good all the time; and all the time, God is good." Sometimes it just takes us a little longer to fully realize the extent of that statement. Sometimes we may not know the "reason" until we meet those children again.

Old Bibles

Occasionally I find someone's old <u>Bible</u> at a yard sale or an auction. Most of the time when that happens I buy it so that it will have a good home. Often the pages are old and yellowed and the cover is crumbling. Sometimes some of the scripture verses are highlighted or underlined. What I like most is when I find an old <u>Bible</u> that has personally written notes in the margins. Then I know that someone at some time loved that particular copy of God's Word. I think how it must have comforted and encouraged someone.

In a way it is sad that no one in that person's family wanted to keep the Bible. Perhaps there were no family members left, but more than likely there were and they just did not want the Book. That is very sad to me. I hope and pray that, when I die, someone will cherish my Bibles then as much as I do now. I also hope that some of them are falling apart from wear and tear by the time I leave them behind.

How often do we treat our Bibles as objects on an auction block? What are they worth to us---fifty cents or a dollar? In today's world many people seem to feel that way. Our Bibles are made of paper and ink, but God's Word is actually a living, breathing, immortal object. It will never pass away. It is priceless.

PSALM 119:105

Your word is a lamp to my feet and a light for my path.

1 PETER 1:24-25

For, "All men are like grass, and all their glory is like the flowers of the field; the grass withers and the flowers fall, but the word of the Lord stands forever."

A Few Sour Notes

The piano lessons that I took many years ago are, in a sense, a blessing and a curse (as Monk would say). I play the piano a little bit; at least I can read music. As we move from place to place with my husband's job, we always find a church that makes us feel "at home." Sometimes there comes a nighttime service in which the pastor will ask the frightful question, "Is there anyone here who can play the piano? Our regular pianists are all absent tonight."

What is there to do in a situation such as that? I know that I am very out of practice where a piano is concerned. I used to play enough to do a decent job of it, but that was many years ago. My mind begins to battle within itself. Should I just keep my mouth shut, sit quietly and safely in my seat, and sing accappella with the rest of the group? Somehow that makes me feel like a liar in God's very house. Should I "fess up" and admit that I can play a little bit, and risk humiliation, as my fingers are likely to strike some sour notes as the congregation tries to sing to my pitiful accompaniment? That would be the "honest" thing to do, and that is what I invariably end up doing. It is a long walk to that piano. Often the people sitting in the seats barely know who I am because we are new to their community, but they are kind and seem to appreciate my feeble endeavors.

I wonder why God keeps putting me in that position. He could enable me to play beautiful music without those sour notes, but He doesn't. I always hit a few of them, but I do my best. As I have pondered this situation, I have come to the conclusion that all I can do is my best, and that is all He requires. The sour notes keep me humble. Admitting I can play the piano, even though it makes me extremely uncomfortable to do so, keeps me honest. Knowing that He and the people singing love me "sour notes and all," keeps me thankful.

Life is full of sour notes. God allows them because they help us grow in character and faith. The harmony in our lives comes from our relationship with our Father, not from life's circumstances. He can take our sour notes and turn them into a beautiful melody.

David told the leaders of the Levites to appoint their brothers as singers to sing joyful songs, accompanied by musical instruments: lyres, harps and cymbals.

Right or Left

MARK 10:35-39

*Then James and John, the sons of Zebedee, came to Him. "Teacher,"
they said, "we want you to do for us whatever we ask."
"What do you want me to do for you?" he asked.
They replied, "Let one of us sit at your right and
the other at your left in your glory."
"You don't know what you are asking," Jesus said. "Can you drink the
cup I drink or be baptized with the baptism I am baptized with?"
"We can," they answered.*

LUKE 23:33

*When they came to the place called the Skull, there they crucified him
along with the criminals---one on his right, the other on his left.*

James and John had no idea just what they were asking when requesting to be placed on the right and left of Jesus. They envisioned a glorious earthly kingdom. Christ knew there was much suffering ahead.

As John witnessed the crucifixion, I wonder if he finally understood the full impact of what Christ had tried to tell him. He and his brother James were soon to learn what it meant to follow Christ. James became the first of the disciples to be killed for the cause, and John was later exiled on the Island of Patmos and tortured in various other ways.

All of the disciples finally learned that the kingdom about which Christ spoke was unlike any other kingdom they could imagine. He is not like what the "world" perceives as a "king." Whether they (or we) sit on His right or His left makes no difference. We should be thankful to just sit at His feet. Our only desire should be to dwell in the presence of our King. As the saying goes, "We must get 'right' or be 'left' behind." That is the only "right or left" about which we should be concerned.

SATAN

1 Peter 5:8

Be self-controlled and alert. Your enemy
the devil prowls around like a roaring
lion looking for someone to devour.

SATAN WENT FISHING

Old Satan went out fishing for wayward souls of men,
And many helpless people were caught in nets of sin.
His bait was earthly pleasure; his lures were greed and pride.
He fished with lies and promises with nets flung far and wide.

Satan's hook looked tempting, but soon it became clear
That looks can be deceiving, and doom was lurking near.
The fish were hooked completely; it seemed they could not win;
So Satan felt secure as he calmly reeled them in.

Suddenly the water began to rise and fall,
And some of Satan's fish began to hear God's call.
Christ came down to earth and cut Satan's safety chord.
Satan screamed in terror as he fell overboard.

Satan thought the fish and seas all belonged to him,
And for a while it seemed man's hopes were growing dim.
Suddenly the devil's fate became dark and grim.
Jesus overturned his boat, and Satan could not swim.

---

2 CORINTHIANS 11:13-15

For such men are false apostles, deceitful workmen,
masquerading as apostles of Christ. And no wonder, for Satan
himself masquerades as an angel of light. It is not surprising,
then, if his servants masquerade as servants of righteousness.
Their end will be what their actions deserve.

SATAN'S LIES

Satan is a handsome thing that comes in many forms;
He promises all sunshine, but what he brings are storms.
He says things we want to hear like, "Just this once won't hurt."
He loves to see God's children wallowing in the dirt.
"Everyone is doing this," are favorite words of his.
At making sin sound tempting, he's really quite a whiz.
"You owe it to yourself---you deserve to have some fun.
It's just some worldly pleasure; now what harm could be done?
No one will know; no one will tell; you'll get by with this.
Go ahead and take that leap; I'll catch you if you miss.
You work so hard you know you need a little pleasure.
I can give you satisfaction and all Earth's treasure."
Old Satan has become a most proficient liar;
He's seeking souls to add more fuel to his fire.
But Satan makes those promises just to bait his trap;
He makes it sound enticing to step across the gap.
He wants to separate us all from our Lord above
And give us worldly treasures in place of God's true love.
Satan is a jealous one, but so is God our King;
We cannot serve two masters and hear the angels sing.
We must beware when Satan comes knocking on our door,
For he cannot gain entrance if his words we ignore.
He knows our weakest moments and every great desire.
He says that anything we want he will help acquire.
Temptation of any kind old Satan will employ.
He doesn't plan to help us; his goal is to destroy.
The gifts that he can give us are temporary things;
The only thing eternal is what salvation brings.
So just say no to Satan, and he must go away.
Listen for the Father's voice, and in His shelter stay.

LUKE 16:13

"No servant can serve two masters..."

JAMES 4:4

...Anyone who chooses to be a friend of the world becomes an enemy of God.

Sneak Attack

The devil tried to get inside my head
Before I got my body out of bed.
He tried to fill my mind with fear and dread
Before my morning scripture had been read.

I told him that he had to go away;
He could not hang around and ruin my day.
I'd pay no heed to what he had to say;
He would not spoil my joy with his decay.

I told him that he was not invited;
That everything from him had been blighted.
Through my Savior all my wrongs were righted;
My darkest alleyways had been lighted.

I told him that I would not play his game;
He would not cripple me and make me lame.
He could not fill my mind with thoughts of shame.
He fled when I called out my Savior's name.

EPHESIANS 6:10-11

*Finally, be strong in the Lord and in his mighty
power. Put on the full armor of God so that you can
take your stand against the devil's schemes.*

Shake the Dust of Regrets

To have regrets in life can be a blessing or a curse;
They can make me do better, or perhaps make me do worse.
When I have sinned, I find my mind filled up with excuses.
I blame it on all those things I think are life's abuses.
I know that all alibis should be put back on the shelf;
When looking where the true fault lies, I must look at myself.
But when I blame myself, that's when regrets control my mind,
And as I search for answers, these two choices I can find.
I can be like Judas who let regrets drive him insane.
He hanged himself because he found he could not stand the pain
Of knowing what he did to one so innocent of blame.
Instead of seeking mercy, he gave in to sin and shame.
Even though I too have guilt of thirty silver pieces
From all the times I've let Him down, my guilt he releases.
Through Jesus' blood all my regrets and all my shame and sin
Are covered and forgotten---now old Satan cannot win
By dragging out my past mistakes. My hopes and dreams won't rust.
Through regrets I've learned a lesson, now God says, "Shake that dust!"

MATTHEW 27:3-4

*When Judas, who had betrayed him, saw that Jesus was
condemned, he was seized with remorse and returned the
thirty silver coins to the chief priests and the elders. "I have
sinned," he said, "for I have betrayed innocent blood." "What
is that to us?" they replied. "That's your responsibility."*

PRAYING FOR SATAN

I wonder what would happen if every now and then
We said a prayer for Satan and hoped his soul to win.
What would he do; how would he feel, if he heard us pray?
When he heard our pleas to God, would he just run away?
It seems, after all this time, that he would realize
The choices that he once made just were not all that wise.
What would God think? Would He approve? Oh, just what should we do?
We're told to pray for lost souls. Does that mean Satan, too?
God says to pray for sinners, so Satan qualifies.
I wonder if he's sorry behind his gruff disguise?
He'd already lost the battle as soon as he fell.
He knows his destination is surely straight to hell.
He strove to rise the highest, but fell short of the mark.
Instead he is the lowest and hiding in the dark.
Can he regret his choices somewhere down deep inside?
Perhaps can he be sorry for arrogance and pride?
If he had one more chance to live with God in glory,
Would he change? Could he change? Or be the same old story?
Something just made me wonder---would it be wrong or right
If I included Satan in my prayers tonight?

NOTE: Satan does not have a soul to save!!!

OTHERS

Matthew 22:37-39

Jesus replied: "Love the Lord your God with all your heart and with all you soul and with all your mind. This is the first and greatest commandment. And the second is like it: 'Love your neighbor as yourself.'"

THE NURSING HOME

Some were waiting for us when we entered through the door.
As we prepared the program, we were joined by a few more.
We came from different churches, praying that we could
Remind them of a Father who's so loving and so good.
We passed out hymnals all around, though soon we could tell
That no one really needed books, they knew those songs so well.
Even though the years had weakened bodies and dimmed eyes,
The lilt of faithful voices still rose up and reached the skies.
Their love of God was evident; they were not ashamed
To tell us of their love for Him. His power they proclaimed!
I imagined how their Bibles must be old and worn
From the hours they spent reading from dark of night 'til morn.
We could learn much more from them than we could ever teach
Years of love and knowledge sat there right within our reach.
Their faith, their lives, their children, they're willing to discuss.
We went there to serve them, but they ministered to us!

LEVITICUS 19:32

*Rise in the presence of the aged, show respect for the
elderly and revere your God. I am the Lord.*

BUT FOR THE GRACE OF GOD

While leaving a busy mall after Christmas shopping one December day, I was held up in a small traffic jam while waiting to exit onto the highway from the mall parking lot. As I waited patiently in the line of automobiles, I could see a shabby, downcast man standing beside the exit. He held a cardboard sign with the words "Hungry Vet" written across it. I know that some people do not believe in giving cash to such people because it is thought that they will use the money for drugs or alcohol, but I always try to give them a few dollars in case they really are hungry. What they actually do with the money is between them and the Lord. If I have the right intentions in my heart when I give, then that is between my Lord and me.

It always crosses my mind whenever I see someone in that position that I could be the homeless person on the street, or perhaps it could be someone I love. Nothing in this world is certain as far as financial security is concerned. As the old saying goes, "But for the grace of God go I."

As I thought about that man later, I realized that we are all "beggars" in one way or another, especially where our salvation is concerned. God did not have to give His Son to pay for our salvation. No one could have forced Him to do so. He gave because of the love He has for all of us. Like the widow's mite, He gave the best He had out of the goodness of His heart. Now it is our turn to give, not just money, but love and forgiveness and our testimonies of salvation so that others may know of His sacrifice.

As we travel along this life's road, let us never forget what we beggars have received from our Savior---Amazing Grace.

HEBREWS 4:16

Let us then approach the throne of grace with confidence, so that we may receive mercy and find grace to help us in our time of need.

A Beggar on the Street

I saw a man standing beside a busy road;
Etched into his face were all the debts he owed.
The sign he held proclaimed he was a "hungry vet,"
And in his eyes were scenes that he could not forget.
I rolled down my window with cash for him to spend;
The things he had been through, I could not comprehend.
At first he did not see the help that I held out;
His gaze went to some place I could not know about.
I made a sound and then his head turned in surprise.
I never will forget what I saw in his eyes.
A lonely, tortured soul stood by that road that day---
One more of God's children trying to find his way.
"Have a Merry Christmas. May God bless you," he said.
I wanted to help him, but he blessed me instead.
For all of us mortals must bear our scars of sin
And struggle through battles that we alone can't win.
God rolled down His window so sin He could defeat;
He offered salvation to us beggars on the street.

1 SAMUEL 2:8

*He raises the poor from the dust and lifts the needy from
the ash heap; he seats them with princes and has them
inherit a throne of honor. "For the foundations of the earth
are the Lord's; upon them he has set the world."*

THE PRISONER

She sits inside a prison after years of sin and strife
And thinks about mistakes she's made and how she's ruined her life.
She never had much chance to learn the facts of right from wrong.
No one was there to comfort her through nights so cold and long.
For years she's wandered through this world just searching for some peace,
Not knowing of a God so great who offers sweet release
From worldly things that weigh her down and will not let her go.
There is a King who died for her, and we must let her know!
We'll hear these words when at His throne we bow on bended knee,
"As you have done for those I love, you've done so unto me."
We all have sinned and could be bound in Satan's private jail.
But for the grace of God, we would be sitting in a cell.

MATTHEW 25:39-40

"When did we see you sick or in prison and go to visit you?"
The King will reply, "I tell you the truth, whatever you did for
one of the least of these brothers of mine, you did for me."

OUR SOLDIERS

Father, there are many soldiers kneeling down in prayer.
I know it brings them comfort to know that you are there.
They face a situation such as they've never known;
Brave men and women in a war, though some are scarecely grown.
Their families wait patiently with hope and trust that you
Will love, protect and guide them and bring them safely through.
On foreign soil so different from what life used to be
They place themselves in danger to keep our country free.
While we are safe at home sleeping snuggly in our beds,
Often on the cold, hard ground is where they lay their heads.
Some recall a country where deer and antelope roam,
While some remember cities or cotton fields back home.
Their backgrounds may be different, but when they heard their call,
Each went to serve his country---each willing to give all.
Because they love their homeland, the fires of home still burn.
With love and pride and thanks, we await their safe return.

PSALM 71:5-6

*For you have been my hope, O Sovereign Lord, my confidence
since my youth. From birth I have relied on you;...*

GOD'S CHURCH

God's church is not constructed of mortar and of stone;
It's made of living tissue, of human flesh and bone.
Bricks and wood can never show God's love or lend a hand
To those enduring trials as they pass through this land.
A building cannot reach out two arms to give a hug
Or feel the Holy Spirit give its heartstrings a tug.
It can't wipe away the tears when hearts have been broken
Or hear with understanding words that are unspoken.
A building cannot witness to souls all lost in sin
And tell about a Savior who wants their souls to win.
When Christians stand united against the gates of Hell,
There's no stronger force on earth, and Satan can't prevail.
God's church consists of people, and each one plays a part.
There is but one condition---God's love in every heart.

ACTS 20:28

*Keep watch over yourselves and all the flock of which the Holy
Spirit has made you overseers. Be shepherds of the church of God.*

REMEMBERING

I think of you each time I hear the rain
Playing drums against my windowpane.
I think of you with every ray of sun
That's sent by God before each day's begun.
I think of you on days that end in "y"
And wonder why so soon you had to die.
I think of you each moment, that is true,
For everything still makes me think of you.

PSALM 27:4

*One thing I ask of the LORD, this is what I seek: that I may
dwell in the house of the LORD all the days of my life, to gaze
upon the beauty of the LORD and to seek him in his temple.*

SONGS OF PRAISE

ISAIAH 38:20

The LORD will save me, and we will sing
with stringed instruments all the days of
our lives in the temple of the LORD.

WHEN THE WORLD SEES ME

Verse 1

When the world looks at me,
Lord, don't let them see
This mound of flesh and bone.
Let them see deep inside,
Lord, where you reside.
Let them see you alone.

Chorus:

Lord, don't let them see
Just the human in me
Or just the bruises and strife.
Let them see your face
And a glimpse of your grace
And how you have changed my life.

Verse 2

Let the people I meet
Along this world's street
Notice I'm not the same.
All my sin's washed away;
I am free today.
My Savior took the blame.

Repeat Chorus

Verse 3

There are people out there
Who need me to share
The love I've found in you.
Lord, let my mission be
To tell all I see
How you have brought me through.

Repeat Chorus

HE TOOK IT PERSONALLY

Verse 1

The devil asked, "Jesus, why would you give
Your life for someone who's not fit to live?
These humans are worthless---why should you try?
To win their redemption, you'll have to die!"
Satan said, "Jesus, you do not need them.
They gripe and complain; the whine and condemn.
Why are you willing to die on a tree?"
Then Jesus said, "It's because they need me."

Chorus:

He took the pain
His blood made the stain.
He paid the price
As they rolled the dice.
His flesh was torn
As our sins were borne.
He died for you and for me;
He took it personally.

Verse 2

Satan said, "Christ, why not just let them go?
Why can't you just let them reap what they sow?
Why should you suffer extreme agony?
Why don't you just give them all up to me?"
Christ said, "You devil, they are now in your trance,
And without my help, they won't stand a chance.
They must have a choice to stay or go free.
You may not care, but they matter to me."

REPEAT THE <u>ENTIRE</u> <u>CHORUS</u>.
<u>ADD</u>: Christ took it personally.

ANGELS UNAWARE

MATTHEW 26:34-40

*Then the king will say to those on the right, "Come, you who
are blessed by my Father, inherit the Kingdom prepared for
you from the foundation of the world. For I was hungry, and
you fed me. I was thirsty, and you gave me a drink. I was a
stranger, and you invited me into your home. I was naked,
and you cared for me. I was in prison, and you visited me."*

*Then these righteous ones will reply, "Lord, when did we ever see you
hungry and feed you? Or thirsty and give you something to drink?
Or a stranger and show you hospitality? Or naked and give you
clothing? When did we ever see you sick or in prison, and visit you?"
And the King will tell them, "I assure you, when you did it to one of
the least of these my brothers and sisters, you were doing it to me!"*

Verse 1

He sat along the roadside; a tear shone in his eye.
No one seemed to see him as people passed him by.
His clothes were dirty rags---worn-out shoes on his feet.
I wondered just how long since he'd had a bite to eat.
He shivered in the cold, but no one seemed to care.
Someone else could help him; there are shelters
everywhere.
Something about this man just would not let me go.
Hurt and disappointment had bowed his head down low.
I helped him to his feet and took him home to rest.
Suddenly I wondered, could this have been a test?

Did I just see Jesus all alone by the road?
Was He waiting for me to help carry his load?
Did He seek compassion, maybe one thoughtful deed?
Did I just see Jesus as a person in need?

HEBREWS 13:1-2

*Let brotherly love continue. Be not forgetful to entertain strangers;
for thereby some have entertained angels unawares. (KJV)*

Verse 2

He sits on a park bench and watches others play;
This is now his pastime almost every day.
Perhaps he is the new kid who just does not fit in.
Perhaps he is the bad boy whose life is filled with sin.
His legs may be crippled through no fault of his own.
His home may be violent where grief and pain are sown.
It may take him longer to figure out some things.
His clothes may be shabby beneath those angel wings.
One little girl walks up and helps his heart to mend,
As she says to the boy, "I'd like to be your friend."

Did I just see Jesus? Was He longing to be
Part of that happy group running wild and carefree?
Was He that little girl with a heart meek and mild?
Did I just see Jesus in the eyes of a child?

JOHN 14:1-4

*Jesus said, "Do not let your hearts be troubled. Trust in God;
trust also in me. In my Father's house are many rooms; if it were
not so, I would have told you. I am going there to prepare a place
for you. And if I go and prepare a place for you, I will come
back and take you to be with me that you also may be where
I am. You know the way to the place where I am going."*

Verse 3

The doctor's face was grim; the report was not good.
He tried so to be brave, and we all knew he could.
He listened to the words with loved ones by his side.
In the weeks that followed, we know he sometimes cried.
He loved his friends and family and did not want to leave.
He could not bear to know how much those left would grieve.
He fought a hard battle with eyes fixed on the cross,
But in his heart he knew this battle would be lost.
He closed his eyes to rest, and gently slipped away.
As I sat there, listening closely, I could almost hear him say,

"Oh, I just saw Jesus with his arms open wide;
And as He reached for me, my soul hurried inside.
Now this journey's over; I've no longer to roam.
Oh, I just saw Jesus, and He welcomed me home!"

SOMEWHERE IN TIME

Verse 1
Each time the whip came down on His back,
Christ felt the sting of Satan's attack.
Satan was sure that Christ could not win;
One man could not bear all this world's sin.
Satan was smug and smiled with a sneer.
He was so sure that victory was near;
But Christ was fighting on our behalf.
God in His glory had the last laugh!

CHORUS

What made Him rise each time He fell
As He battled Satan and Hell?
What made Him stumble up that hill
In His quest to do Father's will?
What kept His feet upon that path
In the midst of Satan's vile wrath?
Why did He suffer such disgrace?
Somewhere in time, Christ saw my face.

Verse 2
How could mankind fear someone so pure?
How could such scorn our Savior endure?
It was for us to this world He came;
I know in my heart we're all to blame.
He knew we were all lost in sin's flood;
The only way out was through His blood.
Love such as His is hard to define;
Those hands with the nails should have been mine.

[Repeat entire chorus and add this line:]

On top of that hill, He saw my face.

I WILL TAKE MY STAND

Verse 1

So many seem to think there is no right or wrong,
And I can't help but feel it won't be very long
'Til Christ will come again to claim us as his own.
Then we can worship God while seated 'round his throne.

Chorus

Lord, I will take my stand, though I might stand alone.
My heart, my soul, my mind I long for you to own.
I will arise and shout, "You are the only God,"
And I will walk along the path that Jesus trod.

Verse 2

The day is growing short; the shadow's growing long.
We must spread his Word before our time is gone.
So many souls are lost just drifting out at sea,
And soon they may be lost for all eternity.

Sing Chorus Again.

Verse 3

We cannot fail this test, ignoring God's own call;
We must keep marching on, though we may slip and fall.
God needs his people now to carry on his Word
And never stop to rest 'til all on earth have heard.

Sing Chorus Again.

Add: Yes I will walk along the path that Jesus trod.

MATTHEW 28:19-20

*Therefore go and make disciples of all nations, baptizing them
in the name of the Father and of the Son and of the Holy Spirit,
and teaching them to obey everything I have commanded you.
And surely I am with you always, to the very end of the age.*

DEUTERONOMY 6:5

Love the Lord your God with all your heart and
with all your soul and with all your strength.

FRIENDS IN HIGH PLACES

Verse 1

Blame it all on my sins
And my rowdy friends,
My selfish and mean attitude.
The last one to see
How bad I could be
How most of my life I'd been rude.
Then with some great surprise
I looked into God's eyes
When life forced me down to my knees.
Then I saw the truth---
Knew I'd been so uncouth,
But I had a way to appease.

Chorus

'Cause I've got friends in high places
Where salvation flows and my Lord chases
My sins away, and I'll be okay.
I believe in our Lord's graces
So I won't slip down to Hell's hot spaces.
Oh, I've got friends in high places.

Verse 2

Well, I knew He was right,
I gave up the fight,
And then, I gave Him my heart.
Now everything's fine,
I've made up my mind,
And from Him I'll never depart.
His blood washed me clean
Right there at the scene;
He made me a new man and then
He promised to stay
With me every day
As Savior and also as friend.

Repeat Chorus

From the Cradle to the Cross

VERSE 1:

From the beginning of time, our Lord had a plan
To redeem us from sin---each woman, child, and man.
He knew from the start we could not stand alone,
So He sent His only Son to claim us as His own.

VERSE 2:

Our Savior knew this world would tempt us constantly,
And from the bonds of sin, we'd struggle to get free;
But it would be in vain---no matter how we tried.
We could not break those knots that Satan's hands had tied.

CHORUS:

From the cradle to the cross my Savior traveled.
He suffered through it all to save my soul.
From the cradle to the cross He made the journey,
And suddenly the devil lost control.

VERSE 3

If the wages of sin we ourselves had to pay
There would be no way out, and we would all be doomed,
But in God's own Word He says that He's made a way
Because Jesus came down and our bodies exhumed.

CHORUS:

From the cradle to the cross my Savior traveled;
He suffered through it all to save my soul.
From the cradle to the cross He made the journey,
And suddenly the devil lost control.

Yes, suddenly old Satan lost control.

JOHN 3:17

*For God did not send his Son into the world to condemn
the world, but to save the world through him.*

THE END

Romans 10:17-18

Consequently, faith comes from hearing
the message, and the message is heard
through the work of Christ. But I ask: Did
they not hear? Of course they did: "Their
voice has gone out into all the earth,
their words to the ends of the world."

FOR CELESTE

Lord, anger flared in me today
And showed my "other side."
I heard what someone chose to say
About things I could not hide.

His nosy self was curious;
He showed no real concern.
His words just made me furious;
They made my stomach turn.

I could hunt him down forevermore
Through east, north, west, or south.
Lord, please reach down and shut that door,
Or, Lord, please shut my mouth.

JAMES 3:6

The tongue also is a fire, a world of evil among the parts of the body. It corrupts the whole person, sets the whole course of his life on fire, and is itself set on fire by hell.

150 YEARS AT LITTLE CREEK
METHODIST CHURCH

October 12, 2003

From my earliest memories this church has been
A rich source of blessings for my friends and my kin.
When I was a child, I loved our Homecoming Day;
We'd all get together to worship, eat and play.
The tables were laden with all kinds of dishes
Much like when Christ blessed the five loaves and two fishes.
We took all for granted, never stopping to think
Of the hours each mother stood at her kitchen sink.
The work of our fathers we should count not the least
As they labored long hours to provide such a feast.
But we were just children, and we had not a care;
We had cousins to play with and stories to share.
Now as many years have so rapidly flown
And we have children and grandchildren of our own,
It makes no big difference how far we may roam;
We still seek the comfort of our first Christian home.
Through the years there have been struggles---times have been hard,
But a few of the faithful have stood at the guard.
The doors are still open to welcome us inside
Anytime we need love or a safe place to hide.
It was here that we learned of a wonderful God.
It is here that some loved ones are covered with sod.
Yes, some family members have come home to stay;
Their souls are with Jesus---yet not too far away.
We can feel their sweet spirits; they're hovering near
To help celebrate our one-hundred-fiftieth year.
We've gathered together our Lord's blessings to seek
And to thank Him for blessing our home, Little Creek.

They will make war against the Lamb, but the Lamb will overcome them because he is Lord of lords and King of kings--- and with him will be his called, chosen and faithful followers.

THE AUCTION

The auctioneer held my battered soul.
He said, "This one's used and not worth much.
It needs a master to take control
To teach it discipline, rules, and such.
Who'll start the bidding; someone please do,
Although it's all ragged and worn.
Surely it has some value to you
Though it's somewhat abused and torn."

Satan spoke up with quite a loud voice,
"I may find some use for this thing.
Although it would not be my first choice,
It's a soul with a broken wing.
I guess I could grant a wish or two,
If earthly things you'll accept as pay.
I'll even throw in some pride for you;
I'm feeling so generous today!"

Then in a voice sweet and crystal clear,
Christ said, "You must stop these proceedings.
Let me explain just why I am here;
You see, God has heard this soul's pleadings.
Now this soul is no longer for sale;
The price was paid in full long ago.
I see its beauty and worth so well,
And it still has many seeds to sow."

1 CORINTHIANS 7:23

You were bought at a price; do not become slaves of men.

THE DAY IS NEAR

More and more I feel the time drawing near
For Jesus Christ our Lord to reappear.
Demons are at work; Satan's getting bold.
Things of Earth will pass away as foretold.
Sin is rampant, and fewer seem to care;
Far less warriors kneel to God in prayer.
There are wars and natural disasters,
And many still strive to serve two masters.
Time is short and Satan's in a panic;
Actions prove that he is getting frantic.
We see and hear things we could not have dreamed,
And everyday our Lord's name is blasphemed.
There seems to be so little fear of God,
Of judgment day, or any vengeance rod.
Sin holds on tightly; some will not be budged.
They don't believe one day they will be judged.
Can't people see the time is now to choose?
They must decide; there's everything to lose.
We must not wear the mark of that great beast
When Jesus comes, appearing in the east.

MATTHEW 24:36

"No one knows about that day or hour, not even the angels in heaven, nor the Son, but only the Father."

THE EPITAPH

"He passed away, to no one's regret."
What sadder words could be said?
His body had scarcely turned cold yet,
But no one cared he was dead.

What kind of life must that man have led
To merit that epitaph?
What dreadful deeds and harsh words were said?
A life as worthless as chaff.

How hard a heart beat within his chest?
How tormented was his soul?
Not one to mourn at his final rest
Alone on a grassy knoll.

No matter how long or short your years,
Do not face another dawn
Until you know there will be some tears
Shed for you when you are gone.

---

2 CHRONICLES 21:20

*Jehoram was 32 years old when he became king, and he reigned in Jerusalem eight years. **He passed away, to no one's regret**, and was buried in the City of David, but not in the tombs of the kings.*

OUR HEART'S DOOR

How often will our Savior knock upon the door---
Wait to gain admittance to see our heart's decor?
Are we ashamed to open it and let Him in?
Do we need to clean the cobwebs of all our sin?
Is the room of Care all covered with mounds of dust?
Is the door to Love sealed tightly with years of rust?
Does Compassion have a dwelling place somewhere inside?
Are there things in there we feel an urgent need to hide?
Does Forgiveness have its own room near Mercy, too?
Does Patience sit and look out at a Joyous view?
Does Kindness live by Faithfulness just down the hall?
Do we keep Self-control contained behind a wall?
Have we rearranged our hearts to make some room for Peace?
Are there things locked there that we know we should release?
Gentleness and Goodness need plenty room to grow,
And Thankfulness and Praise have many seeds to sow.
When Jesus knocks on our heart's door, let's open wide
All the rooms and ask Him to please come inside.
Let's have prepared for Him only our very best
And let Him know He's always our most welcomed guest.

REVELATION 3:20

*Here I am! I stand at the door and knock. If anyone hears my voice
and opens the door, I will come in and eat with him, and he with me.*

GALATIANS 5:22

*But the fruit of the Spirit is love, joy, peace, patience,
kindness, goodness, faithfulness, gentleness and self-
control. Against such things there is no law.*

OUR CHOICES

We can eat at a trough or dine with a King.
We can throw all away or gain everything.
We can waste our talents or win even more.
We can rise up and walk or crawl on the floor.
We can choose to be blind or open our eyes.
We can choose not to learn or choose to be wise.
We can grow in good soil or rust and decay.
We can bear much good fruit or wither away.
We can hide in the dark or let our light shine.
We can live with the King or dwell with the swine.
We can tremble in fear or let love cast it out.
We can have complete faith or continue to doubt.
We can choose resentment or choose to forgive.
We can mope and complain or happily live.
We can find our way home or forever be lost.
We can have life for free or pay a steep cost.
We can choose to believe or choose to deny.
We can stay bound to earth or let loose and fly.
We can still be a slave or have liberty.
We can stay in bondage or choose to be free.

DEUTERONOMY 30:15-19

See, I set before you today life and prosperity, death and destruction. For I command you today to love the LORD your God, to walk in his ways, and to keep his commands, decrees and laws; then you will live and increase, and the LORD your God will bless you in the land you are entering to possess. But if your heart turns away and you are not obedient, and if you are drawn away to bow down to other gods and worship them, I declare to you this day that you will certainly be destroyed. You will not live long in the land you are crossing the Jordan to enter and possess. This day I call heaven and earth as witnesses against you that I have set before you life and death, blessings and curses. Now choose life, so that you and your children may live...

ALONG THE WAY

We rush from here to there and seldom stop to see
Those burdened down with care 'cause we're concerned with "we".
You're thinking about "you"; I'm all wrapped up in "me",
As if we have no clue how God wants us to be.

We race on in blindness and seldom stop to do
Random acts of kindness to help another through.
We justify neglect, 'cause we have troubles, too.
We only show respect for just a chosen few.

We live in dread and fear and seldom stop to say
The words someone should hear to help him through his day.
We just don't realize it hurts when we delay,
Ignoring others' cries as we go on our way.

Along the way we could just stop and chat a while.
Along the way we should share laughter and a smile.
We'd be blessed if we would spread joy and love each day.
This life would be so good with Christ along the way.

ACTS 8:26-29

*Now an angel of the Lord said to Philip, "Go south to the road---the desert road---that goes down from Jerusalem to Gaza." So he started out, and **on his way** he met an Ethiopian eunuch, an important official in charge of all the treasury of Candace, queen of the Ethiopians. This man had gone to Jerusalem to worship, and **on his way home** was sitting in his chariot reading the book of Isaiah the prophet. The Spirit told Philip, "Go to that chariot and stay near it."*

STONES WILL CRY OUT

God will be praised someway somehow;
Before Him every knee shall bow.
We're told to go and spread His love
And tell of grace from up above.
We should tell of things He's done
And share with all about His Son.
We're told to go and testify
How through His grace we'll never die.
For we were born to give Him praise;
He loves to hear our voices raise.
As we are filled with His Spirit,
We want the whole world to hear it.
If we neglect to praise His name,
He will be praised still all the same.
Of this one thing, please have no doubt,
If we don't speak, stones will cry out.

LUKE 19:37-40

*When he came near the place where the road goes down the
Mount of Olives, the whole crowd of disciples began joyfully
to praise God in loud voices for all the miracles they had seen:
"Blessed is the king who comes in the name of the Lord!" "Peace
in heaven and glory in the highest!" Some of the Pharisees in
the crowd said to Jesus, "Teacher, rebuke your disciples!"*
**"I tell you," he replied, "if they keep
quiet, the stones will cry out."**

221

HUMAN ERRORS

Abraham refused to wait, although God said he should.
Moses said he could not speak, although God said he could.

Elijah ran for his life and said he'd had enough.
Even Peter failed his test when questions got too tough.

Jonah tried to run away from what God said to do,
And Jacob stole his birthright for just a pot of stew.

Christ's disciples fell asleep when He asked them to pray,
And Samson let Delilah take all his strength away.

Paul himself refused to see 'til scales covered his eyes,
And some of David's choices turned out to be unwise.

Zacchaeus cheated others and was despised by all,
And Eve and Adam messed up and led to man's downfall.

Our God wants to assure us that He will guarantee
That though we are not perfect, He still loves you and me.

DANIEL 9:9-10

*The Lord our God is merciful and forgiving, even though we have
rebelled against him; we have not obeyed the LORD our God
or kept the laws he gave us through his servants the prophets.*